The AAA Bathhouse:from fathers to sons

By:Anthony Hawkins

ISBN:978-1-300-21929-3

Cover Art By Anthony Hawkins

Dedicated to the gay and lesbian community.

Prologue

Anthony managed and owned one of the countrysides best bathhouses in the state. He made most of his earnings from the establishment.

His life was filled with wealth and honor, but he was burdened with a dark secret, a secret that would cause him his marriage. Anthony started his business a year after his departure from a small town college.

He was well respected in the small town,until his secrets caught up with him.Anthony didn't just run a bathhouse,but a gay bathhouse,something the town wasn't quite ready for.

He had joined in,on the events that took place within the walls of the AAA bathhouse,and so did some of his colleagues.The news covered the town,like thick smoke,causing his ten year marriage to crumble.

Anthony fathered one son with his ex wife of ten years,before they were married.He and his ex wife conceived their first and only son when they were only fifteen,giving the town something to gossip about.

But this new information about Anthony shocked the town,but multiplied his profit.Most of the people in town,mainly the men,who complained about having a secluded gay bathhouse near the town,became the AAA's main customers.

Anthony regained his status,showing brutal honesty and loyalty to the town,even after being ridiculed,about his affairs.Anthony was a bold and tough man,shutting down anyone who criticized him about his personal and professional life,the town respected that,but they didn't respect the pain he caused his wife years ago.

Anthony's son was adored by the town,and was no longer a boy,but a man.Anthony had named his son Antonio.He named his bathhouse AAA,wanting to turn it into a family business,wanting each of his descendants to have a name that began with the letter A.

Chapter 1

Anthony brushed the waves in his hair,and then buttoned up his silk shirt.

This was a big day for him,the day he showed his son the ropes.Anthony wasn't sure if his son would approve of his line of work,but it was worth a try.Anthony headed to his sons room,waiting outside his sons door.

Are you ready for your old man to show you your future business? Anthony chuckled.Yea,almost,Antonio chuckled,as he exited his room.Let's get moving then,you taking a damn hour to get ready,you just like me,Anthony chuckled as they headed to an old truck.

Naw,not exactly like you,i dont make a huge salary,and still continue to drive this beat up shit,Antonio chuckled.Your grandfather gave me this car,family is important to me,this truck brings back memories boy,Anthony said proudly.

Anthony started the engine,and then pulled off,heading down the road.Anthony would push the car to it's limits,speeding down the freeway and the grasslands,knowing there were few residents in his part of town.And few police.

Anthony and Antonio arrived at the AAA bathhouse.

Anthony and Antonio both exited the truck,heading towards the entrance.Anthony pulled his arm around Antonio's shoulders,as they entered the building.

Good morning Mr Neilson,a feminine voice spoke.The voice belonged to a man,His eyebrows arched,wearing a brightly colored shirt,and a pair of tan khaki pants.

Is he gay? Antonio whispered to Anthony.Yep,as sweet as a motherfucking piece of taffy,Anthony chuckled in his immensely deep voice.The mans eyes studied Antonio's anatomy.

Is that him? The man questioned.Yea,this is my boy,Anthony said proudly.He favors you,the man said.Hi,im Phil,the man waved.Im Antonio,Antonio said as he nodded his head.

Anthony took Antonio down a huge hallway,until they reached a silent room.The room was clean,and filled with lotions and oils,and stacked with white towels.Strip son! Anthony said quickly.

Strip? Antonio questioned.

Yea,that's what i said,Anthony chuckled.If you say so,Antonio said silently.Stop acting nervous,im your pops,ive seen it all before,Anthony chuckled.

Anthony and Antonio took their clothes off,placing them in a cupboard.I see your jimmy has grown a bit,i remember when it was a tiny little prick,Anthony chuckled deeply.

I see your still staying fit,for an old man,Antonio laughed.Very funny,Anthony chuckled.Let's hit the showers,Anthony said as they entered a cubicle.They both showered for twelve minutes,and then headed back into the room.

Anthony and Antonio grabbed towels from the racks,draping the towels around their waists.Here! Wear these,they keep your feet protected,Anthony said as he kicked a pair of flip flops towards Antonio.Anthony slipped on a pair of flip flops as well.

They both headed down the hall.I wanted to show you this,once you were old enough,Anthony whispered to Antonio.Antonio could hear moans and grunts as they headed down the long hallway.

What in the world is that? Antonio questioned silently as his father guided him down the hall.That's the sound of ecstasy and good hands,Anthony chuckled.

The sounds made Antonio feel nervous and slightly guilty,that,and the fact that he and his father were naked,and only covered with towels,that made his nerves rush throughout his body.

Anthony and Antonio finally reached a slide door,at the end of the hallway.

Anthony slid the door back,letting Antonio enter first.Antonio's eyes widened as he entered the warm room.The room was big,the walls covered with tan tiles,the floor was made of marble,the color of sand.

The room wasn't the only thing that surprised Antonio,the people did also.There were three men interacting with each other,in a way that might offend some onlookers.

Antonio now knew the reason behind the moans and grunts he heard previously.

Anthony stepped beside Antonio,placing his arm around Antonio's waist.Are you pissed at me,Finding out that your fathers a sword fighter? Anthony said nervously,awaiting his sons reaction.

If this is your thing,do you,Antonio said calmly.Im still your son,Antonio said silently.

Anthony's eyes began to water,his sons approval was the only approval he needed.A tall man approached Antonio,his skin a milky brown,his hair freshly cut and perfect white teeth.The mans body was muscular and strong.

You new? The man said seductively.The man bit the edge of his lip,lust filling his thoughts,as he examined Antonio's smooth and toned body.

Come join me in that corner over there,the man whispered.

That's my son Rick,Anthony said with a slight smirk,as he curved his finger towards Antonio.You aint touching this one,this one got my blood running through him,Anthony said softly,letting Rick know that Antonio was off limits.That's Antonio? The man said with a surprised facial expression.Yea! It is,Anthony said smoothly,giving Rick a dirty look.Yep,this my boy,Anthony said again as he gently placed his forehead towards Antonio's,showing Antonio fatherly affection.

My bad baby boy,but damn,you grew up,Rick chuckled.It's cool,Antonio grinned.I guess you finally found out your fathers an ass pumper,Rick chuckled.

Anthony leave that boy alone,let him go over there with the younger kats,Rick grinned.He aint like that Rick,but that dont mean he cant run the business one day,Anthony smiled.

Nigga you know damn well they going try to open that boy up or turn him out,or run that train,you know what i mean,i mean look at the little dude,i was about to get my mack on too,Rick chuckled.

You lucky you told me he was your damn son,nigga i would've made your ass a grandfather,Rick chuckled.

That shit ain't funny motherfucker,Anthony laughed.I would've kicked your ass,for real Rick,Anthony chuckled.It's good seeing you tho youngblood,Rick said,giving Antonio a gentle smile.

Im about to chill over there,Antonio whispered to Anthony.See ya Rick,that's your name right? Antonio said silently.Yea,that's my name,you sexy young buck,call me when your pops start to get on your nerves,Rick chuckled.

Let me know,if you start to feel uncomfortable son,i know this probably aint your thing,Anthony whispered to Antonio.It's cool,do you remember one of the schools i attended,Antonio smirked.

Hell yea,this should be a walk at the park,Anthony chuckled.That shows you that a top notch school doesn't always have top notched students,i almost had to beat one of them teachers asses too,Anthony grinned.Antonio chuckled and then began to explore the AAA.

Antonio went into a corner,sitting on a marble bench,he oiled himself and then laid back.Antonio's eyes shut.

Chapter 2

The hours passed.The sun was no longer in the sky,as Antonio reopened his eyes.

Anthony shook Antonio's arm.Are you up? Anthony questioned.This place is relaxing,but you cant fall asleep here,these guys are hounds,i caught one dude jacking off,while he was trying to touch your manhood,Anthony chuckled.

What? Antonio said as he sat up.You over here sleeping,not knowing this dude was about to blow his shit,while mind raping you,Anthony chuckled.

Your cell phone rang,while you was sleeping,Anthony said as he passed Antonio his phone.You ready to get up outta here? Anthony questioned.I'll stay another two hours,Antonio said silently.

Okay,but im going to play some cards at Rick's house,Anthony said.You my ride,Antonio said.Rick's son will drop you off,Anthony explained.

Alright,cool then,Antonio said.

You know,i tried my best to keep this life away from you,when you were growing up,but i think your able to understand it now,Anthony whispered.

It's cool dad,Antonio said silently.Anthony pat Antonio on the head,and then left.Antonio checked his missed calls.Antonio pressed speed dial,waiting for the person he called to pick up.

A voice answered,as Antonio tightly pressed the phone to his ear.

Hello,this is Tony,what's up? Antonio said quietly.Nigga what took you so long to call me back? The man questioned.I fell asleep,my bad.So,what you up to? Antonio questioned.

Nothing much,what about you? The man said silently.Nothing much,so are we still on for tonight? Antonio questioned.Can we hang out next weekend? I mean,im sort of busy tonight,my cousin Zack is in town.

Yea,ok,cool,i'll call you later then,Antonio said calmly as he ended the call.Antonio's father wasn't the only one interested in men,Antonio had a boyfriend of two years,meeting the youngman when he was in his freshmen year of college.

Antonio knew his boyfriend was lying,his boyfriends cousin had left town two days ago,taking a trip to the canyon.Antonio could feel someone sit beside him,it was a youngman.

What's up dude? The youngman questioned.Nothing much,just chilling,Antonio said nervously.The youngman moved closer to Antonio.You got a boyfriend man? The guy asked.

Yea,i do,Antonio answered quickly.Then why are you here? If you was my dude,you would be at home,getting sexed up,by me,the man said as he licked his full lips.Antonio was very appealing to the youngman.

Antonio chuckled quietly.The youngman was very attractive,his hands strong and firm,his skin a smooth caramel complexion.And eyes that could penetrate through your skull.His hair jet black and curly,cut short.

The youngman was biracial,But his african american roots shined through just as much as Antonio's did.

Im about to head out of here,the youngman said silently.I know it's none of my business,but will you be here next weekend? The deep voiced youngman questioned.

Im not sure,Antonio answered hesitantly.Alright,can i see your phone?

The youngman questioned.Yea,Antonio answered,handing the man the phone.

The man gently grabbed the phone away from Antonio's hand,touching Antonio's arm and wrist,purposely in the process.Here's my number,call me sometime,my names Ricky,The handsome youngman said smoothly in his deep voice.

Antonio smiled gently.Alright,maybe i will man,Antonio said,slightly blushing.

Antonio you have a boyfriend,Antonio thought to himself,trying to resist the temptation of Ricky's charm.

Ten minutes had passed.Antonio saw many things in that short period of time,seeing one man devour another mans well equipped man part.The mans head jerked back and forth,until the other man moaned out,emptying himself into the mans warm mouth.

Antonio saw more men entering the room,men of all colors.

Antonio then turned his head to the right,spotting two men leaning against the tan colored walls,conversing silently.The two mens conversation turned into something more physical than verbal as they began to touch each other.

One of the men groped the bulge in his towel,and then pulled his slightly stiffened penis into full view as he let his towel drop to the shiny marble floor.The man grabbed the other man by the waist,pulling the mans towel from his body as he positioned his exposed penis near the mans face.The man stood on top of a bench as the other man positioned himself under him.

The man slid the mushroom shaped tip of the other mans penis into his mouth,and then worked his tongue around it,as he gagged himself with it.

The man moaned out in pleasure,feeling himself almost being swallowed.Ah,suck that dick,the man whispered,his face switching from facial expression to facial expression as the other man continued to swallow him.

The man pulled his hand around the back of the other mans head,pushing the mans mouth onto him even harder and faster.

Oh fuck! The man grunted,quickly trying to remove the mans mouth from his hard and pulsating penis,before he could explode.

The man shoved the mans hand away,not surrendering the mans penis from his mouth,wanting a taste of the mans nectar.The man exploded,he had exploded in the other mans mouth,his male nectar filling the mans mouth.Eat it up! The man shouted out in pleasure,feeling the wetness inside of the other mans throat.

The man searched the area,as he held the other mans equipment in his firm hands,making eye contact with Antonio,as if he wanted to seduce him.

The man gave the other mans rod one last gulp,as he and Antonio's eyes met.

The other man quivered as he squirted one last shot into the other mans already filled mouth,with a deep grunt,feeding the man his essences.

The man then turned away from Antonio,still cleaning the other mans hard rod with his tongue and mouth,grazing his lips across the tip and shaft,while the other man squirted off again,his loins still throbbing.

Antonio was shocked,seeing the way the men interacted with each other.You ready to go home? A deep voice spoke.It was Rick.Oh,hey Rick,i thought you and my pops left to go play cards? Yea,but your father got tired,mans getting old,Rick chuckled.My son was going to pick you up,but i decided to pick you up myself.

The last time i saw you,you was sucking on a bottle,so what do you suck on now? Rick chuckled silently.

Antonio joined in the laughter.Dont mind me,im an old perve,Rick laughed.But seriously,im sorry if i offended you Antonio,your father would kill my ass,if he knew what i just said,Rick chuckled.

It's cool man,Antonio said quietly.I brought some good stuff,Rick said as he pulled a bottle of hennessy from a brown bag.You want some? Rick said,staring into Antonio's eyes.

Naw,no thanks man,i dont drink much,Antonio replied.Ay! Let me show you something,Rick said,standing to his feet.Alright,Antonio said as he stood up.Follow me,Rick said as he headed to the hallway.

Rick led Antonio to a secluded room,the AAA had plenty of rooms,but this one was empty.Rick sat on the bench,pulling Antonio next to him.Drink man,i wont tell,if you wont,Rick whispered,handing the bottle to Antonio.

Antonio took one sip,and then leaned back.Rick leaned back also,pulling his left arm around Antonio.Five minutes had passed.

Rick smiled as he examined Antonio's facial expression.Rick began to laugh.You fucked up,aint you boy? Rick chuckled.That liquor is getting to you,i can see it in your eyes,Rick chuckled as he moved closer to Antonio,too close in Antonio's opinion.

Antonio's eyes flickered back and forth,his mind began to wander.Antonio was in a trance,dazed from the alcoholic beverage.

Rick pulled Antonio's hand towards his crotch,grazing Antonio's hand across the tip and the edge of his genitals.Rick then slid his hand underneath Antonio's towel,and then began to gently kiss Antonio's neck.

What are you doing Rick? Antonio questioned silently.

Rick shoved his tongue down Antonio's throat,french kissing him,not giving Antonio the chance to talk again.Cool down Rick,Antonio said quietly.

Damn,My bad youngblood,Rick said,while catching his breath.Rick came back to his senses.Damn man,you got me hard as a rock,Rick chuckled silently.Antonio could see the huge bulge pointing from Rick's towel.Rick thought the liquor would make Antonio an easy target,but his plan failed.

Antonio became nervous,his thoughts roaming.Antonio's phone rang,snatching him back to reality.Hello,Antonio answered silently.What's up Antonio,this Eddie,can we hookup the weekend after next? I might be a little busy that weekend too,Eddie explained.

It's cool,whatever,Antonio said.Are you mad? Eddie questioned.Naw,It's alright,Antonio whispered,lying to himself and Eddie.Fuck that motherfucker,Rick whispered to Antonio as he gently pushed Antonio to the bench.

Rick towered over Antonio as Antonio held his phone to his ear.Rick unwrapped Antonio's towel,and then tossed his towel to the floor also.Rick began to grind himself into Antonio.

Antonio moaned out.You alright? Eddie questioned through the phone,hearing Antonio's silent moan.Rick continued to push,his naked flesh against Antonio's naked flesh.Rick was unbothered by the youngman on Antonio's phone.

Rick eased his head towards Antonio's neck,biting gently,and then pushed his lips towards Antonio's,while Antonio was still on the phone.What's that sound man? You smacking in my ear? Eddie questioned in the background as Antonio and Rick continued.

Antonio couldn't resist,he was turned on by Rick's aggressive nature.Antonio dropped the phone,unable to control himself.Deep moans released from the lips of Rick and Antonio.

Rick and Antonio climaxed,three minutes after Eddie hung up.Oh shit! Rick shouted in ecstasy.Damn man,fuck! Antonio grunted in pleasure.

My father would be pissed,if he finds out,Antonio said silently,panting back and forth.I feel you,but look what you did to me,Rick said in a exhausted voice,as he continued to spill himself over Antonio's chest.

Rick's attraction for Antonio was unbearable,he was ignoring the consequences behind his wild lust for Antonio.

Damn man,im messy,Antonio chuckled.That's what the showers are for baby boy,Rick grinned.Antonio and Rick headed to a shower room,where they washed away their quick fling.

Antonio and Rick headed to Rick's car,after finishing their shower,they were ready to head out.Rick and Antonio got into the car.Rick started the car,and then pulled off.

You wanna go to my place? Rick questioned silently.Maybe next time,i have to study,Antonio said in a clear voice.Oh,alright,Rick said quietly,wishing Antonio accepted his offer.So,how old is your son? Antonio questioned.I dont have one,Rick chuckled.

I told your father that,so i could pick you up myself,Rick grinned.I knew his ass would tire out,and i knew he wouldn't approve of my ass picking you up.This your exit,right? Rick questioned as he turned a corner,driving up the highway.

Yea,im a little further up,Antonio said quietly.I haven't been around these parts in awhile,Rick said.You and your pops like it out here? Rick questioned.Yea,it's pretty cool,quiet tho,but it's cool,Antonio explained.

Alright,you home baby boy,Rick chuckled.Thank's for the ride,Antonio said quietly.No problem,Rick replied.Rick grabbed Antonio's arm,before Antonio could completely exit the car.Everything cool? Antonio said with confusion covering his face.

Yea,just get back in,for just second,Rick said seductively.Antonio pulled himself halfway into the car.Rick leaned over,gently kissing Antonio on the lips.Meet me at the AAA tomorrow night,Rick whispered.

I'll try,Antonio said quietly,shutting the car door in the process.Rick pulled off,waving at Antonio as he drove up the road.Antonio Turned to the house,guilt rushing through his body.

Antonio headed to the front door.Who was that? A strained voice murmured.Antonio turned to the direction of the voice.That was a friend of mine,Antonio whispered.I thought

Rick's son was going to drop you off? Anthony said silently.

Oh,he,Antonio broke off mid sentence,thinking of a lie to tell his father.He had to get his tires changed,Antonio whispered.Oh! Anthony said clearly.Anthony couldn't fully see the car or the driver,the night sky didn't help any.

Come on in,Anthony whispered.Anthony was very protective of Antonio.

That boy keeps calling for you,Anthony said as he and Antonio entered the big house.Who? Are you talking about Eddie? Antonio questioned silently.Yea,that's him,Anthony responded.

He sounded worried,Anthony explained.I'll see you later,Antonio said as he headed through a door.The door led into another small house,Antonio had his own personal space,something Anthony had built,the moment he knew he was going to be a father.

Antonio jumped into his bed,browsing through numbers in his cell phone,Ricky's number struck a nerve in him,but he wanted to attend to Eddie first.Antonio stared to the ceiling,while dailing Eddie's number.

Hello,Eddie answered angrily.This Antonio,Antonio said nervously.Antonio? This ain't the Tony i know,Eddie said sarcastically.What happened to your phone? Eddie questioned.I lost connection,Antonio said silently.Oh,alright,Eddie said silently.Antonio and Eddie talked the night away.

Chapter 3

Antonio opened his eyes,the sunrays scorching his pupils in the process.Antonio's eyes were weary,he was still exhausted by the all night long conversation he had with Eddie.Antonio rose from his bed,heading towards the bathroom.

Antonio brushed his teeth,and then took a shower,reminiscing about his trip to the bathhouse.Antonio dried off,after finishing his shower,he then got dressed,sitting on his bed,after he was fully clothed.

Antonio reached for his laptop,placing it in his lap,he then reached for his cell phone,deleting Ricky's phone number,wanting to focus on Eddie,not Ricky or Rick.Rick and Ricky had similar names,but were not related,although they both wanted to date Antonio.Antonio felt guilty about his unfaithfulness to Eddie,so therefore he cut all ties with the other men.Anthony silently knocked on Antonio's door.

Antonio pushed his laptop aside and then rushed to his door,quickly opening it.You ready to hit the AAA baby bear? Anthony said,waiting for Antonio to respond.Yea,cool with me papa bear,Antonio chuckled.

Alright! Let's roll out then youngster,Anthony spoke,as he and Antonio headed outside,locking up on their way out.

Can i take my car? I might drop pass the diner,later on,Antonio explained.That's alright with me,Anthony chuckled.You met a girl,didn't you? Anthony said with a grin.Nah! Just wanna get some fresh air today,you know me pops,it's usually to work and back home,Antonio said quietly.

Whatever,you met some chick,that's what's going on,Anthony chuckled as he entered his truck.Antonio grinned,and then headed towards his silver volvo.Antonio eased into his car,starting the engine,following behind Anthony.

They headed to the bathhouse,where Anthony gave Antonio more insight on the business.The AAA bathhouse wasn't just a place for one on one sex and orgies,but a place to relax and receive hot oil massages,along with other stress relieving treatments.

The minutes and hours passed them by,until they headed out.Im going out of town,for at least a week,you sure you can handle it? Anthony questioned Antonio silently.Yea,im sure,the place will be fine,Antonio grinned.

Im not worried about the bathhouse,im talking about you,Anthony whispered.You know my number,call me if you feel uncomfortable with this alright,Anthony said as he headed towards his truck.

One day you'll be part owner,your names already on the paperwork,you saw it for yourself,just tell me when you're ready,Anthony chuckled as he pulled off into the night.

Antonio took his fathers words into consideration,but was conflicted with the idea.

Antonio got into his car,and then headed to the diner,meeting Eddie halfway.You missed me? Eddie spoke silently as he and Antonio walked from the diner,into the parking lot.

Yea,i have,Antonio said silently.Then let me come to your place tonight,Eddie grinned.I gotta close up the AAA,Antonio chuckled.Eddie chuckled,i still cant believe your father is gay,Eddie said silently.But anyway,how about tomorrow then? Eddie questioned,awaiting Antonio's response.

Alright,tomorrow then,Antonio smiled.

Eddie rushed his lips into Antonio's,before Antonio could enter his car.It's been awhile since you felt that right? Eddie smirked as he released his lips from Antonio's.

Antonio and Eddie had an audience,but paid them no attention.Eddie headed to his car,waving at Antonio as he drove off.Antonio had butterflies in his stomach,thinking of the kiss he and Eddie shared.

Three young men whistled at Antonio as they headed towards him.You into that faggot shit? One guy spoke.You the son of that dude who runs that gay ass bathhouse,i guess it runs in the family,the man spoke in his deep piercing voice.

Antonio paid him no attention as he pushed his keys into his car.You hear me talking to you nigga? The man said as he slightly shoved Antonio.I dont want any trouble,Antonio said silently.

the man was tall,had smooth brown skin and trimmed facial hair.His hair cut short,in a low fade,and almond shaped eyes,the youngmans good looks didn't wash away the fear Antonio had for him.

Do something! the man shouted as he pushed Antonio onto the car,pressing his body against Antonio's.The other two young men watched with smiles on their faces.

Im Duane nigga,im going to make you remember that name,the man said as he pulled a blade from his pocket.

Duane! What are you doing man? His friends questioned.You lucky i got somewhere to be or your ass would be dealt with,Duane said quietly.

Duane slammed his hand against Antonio's car,in an attempt to frighten Antonio.He pushed his forehead towards Antonio's,their lips almost joining.

Antonio grabbed Duane's arm,twisting it,grabbing the knife in the process.Antonio released his grasp of Duane,pushing him towards his friends.Dont ever do that shit again or i will call the police,Antonio spoke with anger.

Antonio didn't want to report the man,he saw potential in everyone,even thugs like Duane.Antonio quickly entered his car,pulling off,heading onto the road.Antonio's nerves cooled down as he approached the AAA bathhouse.

Antonio parked,and then stepped out of his car.Antonio entered the AAA,tossing all of his clothes into a cupboard,washing his fear away.Antonio closedup the bathhouse,but he himself remained,where he soaked in the steam from the baths,this melted his stress away,this also gave Antonio motivation to join the business with his father.

Antonio stared into the moonlight,shining in from the upper window.

Antonio heard a knock at the AAA's front door.He headed to the front door of the AAA,draping a towel around his waist,covering his naked parts.And then slipping his wet feet into a pair of flip flops.

He slightly opened the blinds,peeping through the curtains.

It was dark and rainy,Antonio could barely see the persons face,only their figure.I left something,a deep voice spoke.We're closed,but i can find your missing item for you,and i'll contact you afterwards,Antonio spoke in a friendly voice.

It's important dude! I need it now,the man said impatiently.Alright,i'll give you an hour to search for it,Antonio said calmly as he opened the door.

Antonio didn't put his safety into question,most gay men had far less criminal records than heterosexual men.The man had lost one of his belongings at a gay bathhouse,so Antonio assumed that the man was gay.The mans clothes were soaked.

The man quickly entered,not giving Antonio a chance to see his face.

Antonio headed into a room,sitting on a bench,relaxing his muscles.

I took a quick shower,i been out all day,sorry i didn't ask first,the man said silently as he adjusted the towel around his waist.Antonio was about to discard his towel,but readjusted it back around his waist,being startled by the mans voice.

Did you find what you were looking for? Antonio questioned.Yea,i did,the man answered silently.

Antonio could not see the mans face,the mans face was now covered with a hot rag.It's cool,no problem,make yourself comfortable,i'll be staying here for a little while myself,Antonio said quietly.

Two more men entered the room,drying themselves off.And then pulling towels around themselves.The men looked familiar to Antonio,but he concentrated his thoughts on relaxing.I hope you dont mind? I had my friends waiting in the car,they got impatient,so i invited them in,the man said smoothly.

Antonio was surprised,but he didn't mind.The other two men sat beside

Antonio as the other man pulled the rag from his face.

Antonio's eyes widened.

It was the same youngman that he had previously had an altercation with earlier.The man had followed him.Antonio stood to his feet,after seeing the mans face.I dont want no trouble man,Antonio said calmly.

Hold him down,Duane said silently as he approached Antonio.

The other two men grabbed Antonio by the arms,each one of them holding an arm.Antonio was a gentle man,but still maintained masculinity,and a strong physique.

But the other men were just as masculine,and just as strong,each possessing a well built body,and they also had the numbers.It was three against one.

They pinned Antonio against the marble bench.

You thought you was tough awhile back,when you roughed me up,but im going to show you who run things dude,Duane explained as he towered over Antonio.Im top dog motherfucker,Duane chuckled.Go ahead,beat my ass,you dont have the strength to handle me on your own,so you pull this,Antonio said in anger.

Naw! Im not going to hit you or kill you,im going to do you nigga,Duane said as he leaned his head against Antonio's neck.What the fuck does that mean?! Antonio yelled.

Im going to do you,like a man does a woman,Duane whispered into Antonio's ear.

Duane pulled his hand around Antonio's waist,about to rip off Antonio's towel,but Antonio struggled.What are you resisting for? Ain't you a faggot,just like your father,Duane spoke silently.

Duane pulled his towel from his waist,and then unwrapped Antonio's.Duane reached for a bottle of oil from the cupboard,massaging it onto his loins,he then gently entered Antonio's body.Antonio whimpered silently as Duane gently inserted and forced himself into his body.

Take it like a soldier dude,you wasn't crying when you roughed me up,Duane said in a low moan as he continued.Duane began to kiss the side of Antonio's neck,pushing himself back and forth into Antonio.

Duane we was just suppose to scare him man,One of Duane's friends said silently.Duane focused his attention on Antonio,refusing to answer his friend.Duane enjoyed himself,aroused by thrills and pleasure.

Small tears rolled down Antonio's eyes.That's what i was waiting for,Duane spoke silently as he pushed himself deeper,becoming even more excited.Duane began to moan,and then poured himself into Antonio with intense ecstasy.

You didn't pull out Duane? One of Duane's friends questioned.

Nah,that was something i gave him to remember me by,Duane moaned,catching his breath.Did You like it,you faggot ass nigga,Duane said,leaning his head towards Antonio's neck,his breath beating against Antonio's skin.

Damn,that shit was tighter than pussy,Duane moaned as he stood to his feet,his genitals still erect.

Damn Markus,you hard as a rock,you wanna fuck him too,Duane smirked.Markus nodded his head in silence,his face filled with agreement.

Let his ass go,Duane ordered.

Antonio quickly pulled his towel around his waist,backing into a corner,in a defensive stance.Dont fuck him Markus,get that mouth action,i know he good with that pretty little mouth of his,Duane whispered.

Get on your knees man,or we are going to fuck you up,Markus ordered Antonio.I want some of that man,Duane's other friend demanded.Go fuck that face then Jim,Duane chuckled.

Markus and Jim surrounded Antonio,each one of them pulling their erect man parts from the opening in their towels.Markus slapped his equipment across Antonio's face,while Jim did the same.

Markus swirled his man part around Antonio's chin and lips,and then penetrated Antonio's mouth with it.Gag on that shit nigga! Markus shouted in pleasure as he fed Antonio his manhood item.

Markus fed Antonio for twenty minutes,until Antonio felt a warm substance enter his mouth,followed by Markus's deep grunts and moans.

Oh fuck yea,Jim said as he witnessed the intense pleasure Markus forcefully received from Antonio.This Dude give better head than Roxanne,Markus boasted.Markus's manhood slipped from Antonio's lips,something Antonio approved of.Put that shit back in your mouth nigga,Markus spoke as he shoved himself back into Antonio's mouth.

You like that homeboy,i bet you like having a whole gang of niggas slut your bitch ass out,Markus grinned,gently caressing Antonio's face.Nigga got skin as smooth as a baby's,Markus chuckled.

They spoke ill of Antonio's sexual preference,but they enjoyed taking advantage of a youngman,they were highly conflicted within their own sexual identities.They used Antonio as a way of fulfilling their secret desires.

Cant talk? Mouth full huh,Markus grinned as he removed himself from Antonio's mouth.Jim slid himself into Antonio's mouth,after Markus evacuated it.

Jerk it,Jim ordered as he placed his prick above Antonio's cheek.Antonio began to stroke Jim back and forth.Markus joined in,his equipment already naturally lubricated from his first encounter with Antonio.

Antonio stroked them both,at the same time,as they dropped their towels to the floor.Jim pushed his crotch deeper into Antonio's firm hands.Jim's prick began to throb as he moaned out,soaking Antonio's warm naked flesh.

Antonio punched Jim in the sack,and then quickly ran from the room.

Chapter 4

Antonio escaped into the woods,his towel falling from his waist as he continued through the trees.

If you tell anybody we are going to kill you nigga! Duane and his group yelled in the background.Antonio approached a small lake,rinsing his mouth with the water,splashing the water on his naked body,wanting all traces of the young men to be gone.

Antonio feared going back home,so he slept in the forest the entire night.Antonio woke up the next day,his nude body in fetal position,slightly covered in dirt and grass.

Antonio jumped to his feet,running back to the AAA bathhouse,he didn't care if Duane or Markus or Jim was still there,he could only think of revenge.He entered the AAA,his face filled with anger.

Some of the things that Duane and the others did to him were things he and Eddie never tried.Antonio hopped into the shower,thoroughly washing away any part of Duane and the others.

He used nearly an entire bar of soap,scrubbing himself with force.Antonio dried himself off,after he finished.Antonio got dressed and then drove home.Antonio chose not to call the police,he wanted to take matters into his own hands.Antonio headed into his room,after reaching his home.

Antonio paced back and forth,his nerves jumping.You're a grown man,pull your shit together,Antonio whispered to himself.Antonio grabbed a knife from the dishwasher,hearing thumps against the front door of the house.

Antonio was secretly wishing that the person at the door was indeed Duane or Markus or Jim,so he could pursue his revenge at that very moment.

Antonio answered the door,it was Eddie.

You alright?! You look pissed off,Eddie explained.Can i come in? Eddie asked.Yea,Antonio replied quietly.You okay? Eddie questioned.Antonio quickly shut the door and locked it.

What the fuck you got that knife for? Did i piss you off or something? Eddie chuckled.Nah,i was chopping something,Antonio responded silently as he put the knfe away.Oh! Eddie replied.I got us some movie tickets,we got three hours before the movie starts,what you wanna do,until then? Eddie said in a quiet voice as he moved closer to Antonio.

Eddie pushed his forehead into Antonio's,and then folded his arms around Antonio's side.Eddie darted his lips towards Antonio's,but Antonio avoided the kiss,his thoughts wandering.

You mad at me dude? Eddie questioned.Naw! Antonio answered,refocusing on Eddie.Antonio pushed his lips into Eddie's,this was one of the most passionate kisses they ever shared.

Antonio truly knew the difference between nice and cruel,Duane and the others taught him that.Antonio grabbed Eddie's crotch as they kissed.Eddie moaned out.

Stop teasing me nigga,you know you aint gonna take it all the way,Eddie chuckled silently.Eddie grabbed the back of Antonio's head,pushing Antonio's lips further into his own.

Antonio's emotions were high,each one of them heightened,this was caused by trauma.Antonio was in a vulnerable state.

Antonio kneeled down,his face nearly buried in Eddie's crotch.Antonio gently pulled Eddie's black denim jeans down,and then pulled Eddie's boxer briefs down,after dropping Eddie's pants.

Antonio slid his tongue across Eddie's growing bulge.What are you doing man?

Eddie moaned out as he bit the edge of his lip.Eddie knew what Antonio was about to do,but tried to play modest.

Antonio pulled his hand around Eddie's waist,grabbing Eddie's rear end,pushing Eddie deeper into the pit of his throat.

Eddie began to moan as Antonio's head jerked back and forth,slowing down and then speeding up.Ah! Damn man,im about to bust,Eddie grunted as he quickly pulled himself from Antonio's mouth.

Eddie let out a deep highpitched moan,as he shot out ounces of his manly functions,soaking his pants and underwear.Damn dude,look what you did to me,Eddie whispered,his heart racing.

You must be horny today baby,Eddie chuckled,breathing heavily in the process.You see what you did to daddy,Eddie moaned out.Antonio began to laugh as he stood to his feet.

That's just akward dude,Antonio chuckled deeply.Not bad,but akward,Antonio chuckled.What? Eddie chuckled.The whole daddy thing,especially me finding out my pops is gay now,Antonio laughed silently.

I been meaning to ask you,did you hookup with anybody in that bathhouse joint? Eddie questioned silently as he pulled his boxers and pants back up.Antonio became silent.Nah,what makes you say that? Antonio whispered,feeling guilty about the lie.

Because i know alot of dudes use those places as a hookup party,Eddie murmured.I dont know how i would handle you doing what you just did to me,to somebody else,for real nigga,Eddie chuckled.

Just the thought of you giving somebody else that feeling,gets me heated man,Eddie said with conviction.Antonio laughed.Nah,that shit aint funny,im serious,Eddie whispered,Eddie meant what he said.

Im going to be honest with you,something happened,Antonio said silently.What the fuck you mean something happened nigga? Eddie said with frustration.It was this dude name Rick,he's a friend of my father,Antonio said timidly.

Nigga you a slut ass motherfucker man,to be truthful,nigga i actually have feelings for your ass,i fucking loved you nigga,i still love you homey,but that's some fucked up shit man,that's grimy cuz,Eddie spoke in his deep angered voice.

A friend of your father,how old is he? Eddie questioned.Around my fathers age,but you know my pops had me with my mother at a young age,so the dude looks kind of young,just like my dad,Antonio explained.

My bad man,i was stupid,Antonio whispered.Naw! It's cool,aint no biggie,im a grown ass man,what the fuck i look like,tripping over another nigga for,Eddie spoke,his eyes red and watery.

Nigga i should wreck your shit,Eddie said angrily,approaching Antonio with his fist balled up tightly.

Eddie pushed his forehead against Antonio's,they were chest to chest,face to face.Dude i should fuck you up man! Eddie shouted,restraining himself from hitting Antonio.Hit me nigga! i already been through enough shit,Antonio shouted.

You still a dude nigga,dont tempt me motherfucker,Eddie said in his deep voice.So that makes it okay? Antonio questioned.Naw,it's never okay to hit someone you love,but im still human nigga,Eddie said,catching his breath.

Im out dude! Eddie shouted as he headed to the front door.Wait man! Antonio shouted,as tears fell from his eyes,as he followed behind Eddie.What the fuck you crying for? Eddie questioned Antonio,not really wanting to see Antonio hurt in any way,even if he was angry with him at the moment.

You did me wrong,Eddie explained as he turned to Antonio,staring him in the eyes.You gave him head or did you let him fuck you? Eddie questioned,eagerly awaiting Antonio's response.

Neither,we were just grinding,nothing serious man,i got pissed,because it felt like you was avoiding me,that's the truth,Antonio explained.And What was that shit you said about going through enough? Going through what man? You never tell me anything,Eddie whispered.

Antonio's thoughts went to a dark place,as he thought about the incident that occured the day before.Antonio banished the thoughts from his mind.Antonio gave Eddie a quick peck on the cheek.Eddie frowned,trying to keep himself from smiling.

You still trying to go to the movies nigga? Eddie questioned Antonio silently.Yea,Antonio said nervously,happy to know that Eddie didn't hold a grudge.I forgive you dude,but you gotta earn my trust again,Eddie explained calmly.

You are going to give me some of that ass when we get back home,Eddie demanded with a smile.Alright,it's whatever,i agree,Antonio smirked.Alright,you agreed nigga,Eddie said as he gave Antonio a quick slap on the backside.They both left out,Antonio locked the house up,as he and Eddie headed to the movies.

They stopped pass Eddie's place,before the movies,where Eddie changed his underwear and pants,before they arrived at the movie theater.

The movie was an hour and thirty minutes long.

Antonio and Eddie cruised the mall,after the movie was finished.Antonio was spotted by many of the people in town.Hey Antonio! Call me when your father switches teams,or if i cant have the father im going for the son,a short woman chuckled.Antonio chuckled in response.

What's up little Antonio? I haven't seen you in ages,how is your father doing? A tall man asked Antonio as he carried three bags.He been cool,Antonio answered.Good,the man responded.

Antonio and Eddie browsed the mall for thirty minutes,and then finally headed out to the car.Antonio was about to step inside his car,until he became distracted by a familiar voice.

The voice brushed across his ears,sending chills through his body.Antonio turned to the direction of the sound,staring Duane in the eyes.

Duane was exiting the mall,with a young woman on his arm.You cool? Eddie questioned Antonio,seeing Antonio's facial expression.Antonio's anger began to swell,his adrenaline scorching through him like fire.

He headed toward Duane calmly,a dangerous calm.Duane's eyes widened,as Antonio approached.Dude look,Duane spoke,unable to finish his sentence,after being hurled to the ground by Antonio.

Antonio began to pummel Duane into the concrete.

The young woman that assisted Duane began to scream in fear.Help! The woman screamed out.Duane's nose began to bleed as Antonio continued to beat him.You a lame ass nigga without your friends huh,Antonio said through his teeth as he pulled his fist back and forth,using Duane as a punching bag.

What's wrong Antonio,what this dude do to you? Eddie questioned silently as he held Antonio by the waist,trying to calm him down.Everyone watched in fear.

Duane's lady friend approached Antonio from the back,about to help Duane,seeing that no one else would.The young woman was yanked by another woman,an older woman,before she could lay a finger on Antonio.

Baby girl stay outta that! That's between men! The woman shouted,as she restrained the girl.Who are you to him anyway? The woman questioned.Im his girlfriend,the young woman answered.You chose Duane Jones to be your boyfriend? The woman said with a surprised facial expression.

Girl that boy is a trouble maker,watch yourself around him,the woman said.Antonio finally let up,rising to his feet,his heart pounding.Antonio felt somewhat relieved,after giving Duane a quick spanking.

Get him outta here,before the police come,i know Antonio,he slow to violence,duane must've did something to piss that boy off,the woman explained.

Eddie quickly placed Antonio in the passenger seat of the car,and then quickly rushed to the driver seat.Im going to kill that nigga man,Duane said in a strained voice,coughing up blood.

It ain't over dude,im going to get in that ass again! Duane yelled,as Eddie and Antonio pulled off.Fuck him,let's go home baby,Duane's girlfriend spoke softly,helping him up off the ground.Get the fuck off of me man! Duane screamed at his girlfriend,holding his mouth,trying to stop the blood from flowing.

Duane and his girlfriend quickly fled the scene,Duane knew he would get himself into trouble also,if he reported Antonio,a man whom he molested.

Chapter 5

Eddie and Antonio hit the highway.

Damn! You fuck that dude shit up! Eddie chuckled.What he do to you? Eddie questioned,hoping Antonio would reply.It's nothing,me and him just had a little misunderstanding,Antonio explained silently,not wanting to explain the entire situation.

Antonio felt embarrassed,thinking it was unmanly to come clean about him being molested by a gang of thugs.

Just drop it Eddie,please,let's just go home,Antonio said quietly.Alright,my bad,Mr beat your ass down in front of the mall,Eddie chuckled deeply,almost losing his grip on the steering wheel.

Watch the road! Antonio laughed out.I didn't mean to raise my fist at you earlier dude,i was just pissed at that moment,i cant handle you fucking with somebody else,Eddie whispered.It's cool,but im not the only guilty one here,Antonio chuckled.What you mean?

Eddie whispered.I know that your cousin wasn't in town,Antonio said silently.

Eddie froze,in shock.

I was kind of horny man,and i started chatting with this dude on mantext,dude wanted me to come over,but i tried my best to resist,Eddie murmured silently.Dude just jacked me off,that was it,Eddie explained.

Sometimes i get impatient Antonio,you be trying to take things slow,but it gets hard for me sometimes,i know we still trying to learn each other,but at least give me more fourplay,Eddie chuckled softly.I hate to say this,but im a man dude,i have needs,im pretty sure you know the feeling too,Eddie said with a serious expression.

Me and you having so much in common,when we get together it should be fireworks,Eddie grinned.I mean sex isn't the most important part in a relationship,but it's next on the list,you barely wanna give me any physical contact,physical contact doesn't always have to be sexual,you know,but you can at least touch me,Eddie said silently.

Sometimes it takes you hours and days to hit me back up,that makes me feel rejected,so therefore i reject your ass,Antonio smiled.I respect the fact that sometimes you might be a little busy,but damn,days tho,Antonio smirked.

My bad man,im going to change that,but sometimes my cup be full,and i dont want that shit to spill on you,you feel me,but we both need to work on this alright Tony,Eddie smiled gently.Now you calling me by my nickname,trying to be smooth huh,Antonio chuckled.

Eddie chuckled deeply.Number one,i dont want you giving your ass and dick or any other part of your body to any other nigga besides me,just because i missed one of your calls or took awhile to respond,i dont care if some nigga dick grazed your hand by accident,that would still kind of piss me off,Eddie smiled softly.

And number two,love me nigga,Eddie smiled.So you taking it there,alright,heres my list,Antonio grinned.I dont want nobody jacking your shit,just because your dick got a little hard that day,Antonio smiled.And number two,love me too,Antonio whispered.

That's a done deal then,Eddie smiled.Eddie smiled slightly,being aroused by something in his thoughts.I know somewhere we can go for the rest of the day,let's go to that bathhouse you and your father own,Eddie said quietly,waiting for Antonio to respond.

It's my fathers,Antonio said silently.Yea,but your name was put on the place since birth,and your pops is begging you to help him run it,Eddie chuckled.

Whatever,let's go then,Antonio responded with a smirk.

Eddie and Antonio headed to the AAA bathhouse,entering through the back door.

Damn this place is big,Eddie spoke,his voice echoing through the quiet halls.How many rooms this joint got?

Eddie questioned.About twenty,including the master bath,Antonio answered.

I bet you see all kinds of shit in this piece,Eddie smiled.Yea,pretty much,Antonio responded.Let's take a tour then,Eddie whispered.Eddie and Antonio entered one of the empty rooms.

Eddie began to read one of the signs on the wall.It Says right there,as big as day,must be nude,or only covered with a towel,Eddie grinned.Eddie knew this meant easy access.

Take them clothes off nigga,Eddie whispered to Antonio.That goes for you too then,Antonio responded.Antonio and Eddie took off every piece of their clothing and then shoved them into a cupboard.

Antonio got a full view of Eddie's naked dark chocalate skin,he and Eddie were nearly the same skin tone.Eddie was a foot taller than Antonio,had wide shoulders and full lips,a neatly trimmed mustache and goatee,and attractive to the eyes.

Eddie wore a durag over his short haircut,Antonio was the only one Eddie occasionally exposed his low wavy fade to,Eddie was a conservative person.Eddie wasn't the type of man some would assume to be gay,neither was Antonio,but some towns people had saw their romantic encounter,outside of the diner.

Eddie tried to focus his attention off of Antonio's naked body,this was one of the few times he got a glimpse of Antonio's nudity.Eddie held his package,keeping himself from becoming aroused.

Antonio and Eddie showered for an hour,and then stepped back into the room,once they were done.Antonio dried himself off,so did Eddie.

Antonio and Eddie pulled towels around their waists,and then slid their feet into flip flops,and then headed into another room,the new room they entered was quiet and secluded,the walls had built in intercoms,playing calming music.

Antonio and Eddie shut the door behind them.Antonio and Eddie grabbed blankets from one of the cupboards,spreading them on the marble floor.

Antonio and Eddie kneeled down,laying to their sides,facing each other.Antonio and Eddie could hear the water pour from the fountain near the huge window,that was the only sound in the room besides their kissing.

Antonio examined Eddie's tight body,wanting every part of him.Eddie stared into Antonio's eyes,lust filling his thoughts.

This is what i call easy access,me and you in our birthday suits,sporting nothing but towels,Eddie whispered to Antonio,his hormones rising.

Yea,i know what you mean,Antonio whispered just as quietly as Eddie.

Eddie moved closer to Antonio,their body tempatures rising.Eddie grabbed Antonio's waist,and Antonio did the same.Their lips met.A gust of air flew through the door as someone entered.

There were two men standing in the doorway,completely naked,holding each other by the waist.One of those men was Anthony,Antonio's father.Anthony's eyes widened as he witnessed his son lying on the floor,tightly embracing another youngman.

Antonio's eyes widened also,seeing his fathers equipment swing back and forth,as he held on tightly to another man.I thought you were out of town? Antonio questioned Anthony.Some things got delayed,but what's this? Anthony spoke,awaiting Antonio's response.Antonio! Are you mimicking me? Or are you really,you know,Anthony broke off mid sentence.Anthony pointed his two index fingers together,making gestures.

Yea,i am pops,Antonio said nervously.Im gay,like you,Antonio smiled gently.Eddie waved nervously.At least you got good taste in men,Anthony chuckled.I dont give a damn if you told me you were a tranny chaser,you still my son,now we can share man problems,Anthony chuckled.

That's your son? I might have to get two for the price of one,Anthony's date replied.Anthony's heart fluttered,this was his dream come true,a son he could actually relate to.

Ya'll do ya'll thing,im going into the next room,Anthony whispered,grabbing his man friend by the backside.

Anthony and his male friend left the room,closing the door on their way out.Damn dude,my heart is jumping,Eddie laughed.I thought your father was gonna kick our asses,Eddie chuckled.

So now what? Antonio questioned silently.Let's finish what we started,Eddie smiled as he began to kiss Antonio.

Anthony and the other man entered the room again.Every room is occupied,can we kick it with ya'll? Anthony questioned.Cool with me,we can just relax and talk,Antonio responded.

No,ya'll dont have to stop ya'll activities for us,push that button on the fountain,Anthony spoke in a clear voice.Anthony moved to the other side of the room,he and his man friend.

Eddie pushed the button.

A large curtain slid through the center of the room,dividing the room into two fragments.

You like it? Anthony whispered.That's cool,both Antonio and Eddie responded.

Antonio could no longer see Anthony or his male friend,the curtains provided privacy.Push the other button on the fountain,Anthony whispered.This time Antonio pushed it.

The music volume went up,and so did every prick in the room.Antonio and Eddie began to kiss passionately,while Anthony and his male friend did the same.

Antonio ripped the towel from Eddie's waist,while Eddie tossed Antonio's towel aside as well,things really got heated after that.Something hit Antonio on his naked rear end,just as he and Eddie were about to move along to step three of their sexual activities.

Antonio reached for the object,it was a condom.

Anthony had slid the condom under the curtains,wanting Antonio to use protection.Antonio was already prepared,but opened the condom anyway,not wanting to waist it.That can be for round two,Eddie chuckled as he kissed Antonio.Alright,but we both get a turn,you'll use one and i'll use one,Antonio smirked.Eddie smiled and then began to kiss Antonio again.Eddie placed his body on top of Antonio's body,pushing his pelvis to Antonio's pelvis,his lips to Antonio's lips.Antonio pulled his arms around Eddie,as Eddie slid the condom onto his fully erect man part.Eddie and Antonio gently became one,breathing heavily as they expressed their love through intense and pleasurable physical acts.

Antonio and Eddie grinded back and forth,making love for hours.Antonio and Eddie switched positions,molding themselves together again,continuing with their sexual bliss.The room was hot and the rods were hard.The moans were loud,but no one could hear,because of the soft music.

No one in the room could hear,but they could feel.Every stroke and every thrust led to an explosive climax,for both parties,Antonio and Eddie,and Anthony and his male friend.

Both father and son enjoyed themselves throughout the day and night.

Chapter 6

Antonio threw away his condom,after releasing his essences into it,he and Eddie were completely done with their love making,they no longer needed the condoms.Damn,we should have brung more rubbers,i wanna round three,Eddie chuckled.Me too,Antonio chuckled along as he and Eddie began to kiss passionately.We out,Anthony spoke as he and his partner headed to the door.Anthony and his man friend left the room first,closing the door afterwards,making sure Antonio and Eddie had their privacy.

Antonio and Eddie remained,kissing and cuddling in the nude.A half an hour had passed.The room door opened slowly,revealing feminine like hands,it was Duane's girlfriend.

She wasn't alone,she was accompanied by Duane himself and Markus and Jim.They entered the room slowly,and confident.No fucking trouble dude! Antonio shouted.

Nah,we here to negotiate nigga,Duane chuckled.Who is this dude? Eddie questioned.The same dude who took my freedom,Antonio said angrily.You still crying over that shit nigga,you probably liked the shit,i bet you busted one on the low,Duane smiled.

Duane's girlfriend had a confused and saddened facial expression,apparently she didn't know that Duane led a double life or she did,but lived in denial.

Look dude,my homey said no trouble,so get the fuck outta here,Eddie demanded,as he stood to his feet,his equipment swinging back and forth.Who the fuck are you,his man or something? Jim questioned.

Yea,you damn right,im his motherfucking man,do something,Eddie said as his nose flared.

Look at the alpha,trying to protect his beta,nigga aint nobody trying to do nothing to him,Duane chuckled.He lucky i dont jump on his ass right now,after that shit he pulled at the town mall,Duane laughed out.

Look,if you keep what happened between us,i ain't snitching nigga,Duane murmured.

What the fuck is he talking about Tony? Eddie questioned as he gently pulled Antonio to his feet.

Hold up,is this the dude you was messing with,the dude you cheated on me with? Eddie whispered to Antonio.

Eddie reached for his towel,wrapping it around his waist.Antonio covered himself with his towel also,as he and Eddie stood side by side.This the dude ain't it? Eddie said with a frustrated expression.

Nah,but like i said,something jumped off between me and him,Antonio said quietly.Leave this motherfucker right now! Eddie shouted at the three men.I will wreck all of you dudes if i have to,that goes for the females too,Eddie said as his muscles flexed.Eddie was ready to defend Antonio,at all costs.

Nah,im a grown man,i can handle myself,Antonio whispered to Eddie,gently holding his arm,not wanting Eddie to fight on his behalf.I dont give a fuck Antonio,a father protects his son,why a man cant protect his mate,Eddie said with a serious facial expression.

Anthony rushed into the room,hearing the commotion.Is everything alright son? Anthony questioned with a puzzled face.Yea,im cool pops,Antonio answered silently.

Nah! You ain't cool,tell your pops what's going on,Eddie demanded.These dudes did something to Tony,he just ain't trying to confess the shit,Eddie explained.What happened Antonio? Im your father,i know when somethings bothering you,you my seed,tell me? Anthony requested silently.

Two tears slowly dropped from Antonio's eyes,as he struggled to hold onto his pride.The dudes ganged up on me,in a sexual way and threatened to kill me,Antonio embarrassingly whispered.

Anthony's face became blank,from the news Antonio told him.Eddie headed towards Duane,but Antonio grabbed him by the waist.Anthony calmly headed out the door,he reentered with three other men,the men appeared to be body guards,all of them dressed in dark uniforms.

Duane and the others were about to leave the area,but was stopped by the body guards.Look man! Im not gay,this is my girlfriend,Duane explained in fear.Your son is lying man,just let us go,Markus explained silently,unsure to what would happen next.

Im outta this camp,Jim spoke as he headed towards the door again.This time the guard shoved him to the marble floor.

Hook them up,Anthony whispered calmly.

The guards placed pulse detectors on all three of the men,starting with

Duane.We usually use these to give people therapeutic massages,and to test their comfort levels,but this shit can also work on liars,Anthony spoke calmly,his eyes puffy and red with anger.

Come here Antonio,Anthony requested,reaching out to his son.

Antonio released his grip of Eddie,as he headed towards his father.Eddie used this to his advantage,punching Duane in the stomach.No,cool down Eddie,i got this,Anthony whispered,keeping his rage concealed.

Eddie kept himself calm,waiting for his chance to attack.

Take off ya'll fucking clothes,Anthony ordered.Duane and the others stripped,removing all of their clothing,their nerves pushing to the surface.Get in the shower,get nice and wet,Anthony explained with a sinister plan coursing through his mind.

Duane,Jim and Markus showered and then headed back out,soaking wet.Duane and the others grabbed towels from the cupboard,wrapping them around their waist as they reformed the line.

I didn't tell none of you punks to get towels,Anthony explained angrily.Jim quickly dropped his towel to the floor,but the others hesitated in fear.

Hook that one up first,Anthony ordered,pointing to Markus.The guards placed a small cord underneath Markus's towel,attaching it to his genitals,they then placed one on the other two,Duane and Jim.

My son is attractive ain't he,Anthony whispered.Look at them full lips,skin as smooth as butter,Anthony spoke,trying to entice the three men.Markus's device began to beep,sending surges to the pulse detector.

Oh,we have a winner,Anthony chuckled.Each time the device beeped,one of the young thugs were hit.I can only imagine what you did with a mouth like this,Anthony whispered.Markus could feel blood rushing to his loins as he fought off Anthony's sexual taunts.

Look how soft and firm his lips are,Anthony continued to taunt.Markus's loins began to stiffen,as he examined Antonio,thinking about the night he forced himself on the youngman.

Markus was soon fully erect,his prick protruding from his towel.Markus wasn't the only one who was solid,Jim was too.

The young men turned their heads to the side,their faces filled with embarrassment.So,i guess ya'll dont swing that way huh? Anthony said sarcastically.

Duane was the only one who fought his urges at that moment,the others gave in.Anthony examined Duane's position.Duane focused on Antonio's smooth and toned abdomen,tightly pressing his legs together.Duane's pulses shot through the roof,causing the machine to beep rapidly.

Spread his fucking legs,Anthony ordered his guards.Duane's manhood stood up,causing his towel to drop.You see that,your boyfriend aint that straight after all,Anthony explained to Duane's girlfriend.

Duane's girlfriend turned her head,not wanting to witness,she secretly knew of Duane's fantasies,but was willing to put up with anything,in order to keep Duane by her side.

Anthony continued to taunt Duane with Antonio's physical presence,until Duane ejaculated spontaneously,without any friction on his part,moaning deeply in the process.

Anthony gave the guards a signal,and at that moment,Duane,Markus,and Jim were all beaten.

Duane's girlfriend watched silently in fear.The water made Duane and his gangs beating much worse.The guards didn't hold back.Duane and the others felt the sting of every blow.

Duane and his group were soon able to leave,but their bodies were sore.

Duane's girlfriend quickly grabbed something out of the trashcan,as she and Duane and the others exited the room,a trashcan that stood near Antonio and Eddie's previous position.No one saw her steal the object from the trashcan,but she indeed placed something into a plastic bag of the sort,and then swiftly tucked it into her purse.

Duane and the woman had planned a silent scheme,only time would reveal it.

Chapter 7

Nine months had passed.

Antonio had finally gave into his fathers wishes,joining the AAA establishment.Antonio and Eddie's relationship had progressed even further within those nine months.

Antonio and Eddie were lying on the bed,in Antonio's room,staring into the stars.Eddie sat up,then eventually stood to his feet.I got something to ask you Antonio? Eddie spoke softly as he pulled Antonio from the big bed.

Eddie slowly placed his forehead against Antonio's,their hearts beating at the same pace.

The room was dim,only lit by candles.You love me right dude? Eddie questioned Antonio.Yea,you know i do,Antonio answered.Man im happy as fuck,when im with you,truthfully,i cant think of anything else,when im around you dude,Eddie spoke with conviction,explaining his feelings for Antonio.

I feel the same way,Antonio replied.

Let's take it to a new level then,Eddie said silently.What do you mean? Antonio questioned,awaiting Eddie's answer.We both admitted that we dont care about what anybody else thinks of us,so marry me Antonio,Eddie whispered.

Antonio's heart dropped.

Marry me dude,Eddie silently requested again,his arms around Antonio.Eddie eagerly awaited Antonio's answer to his proposal,his nerves pushing to the surface.

Antonio opened his mouth,about to speak.

I accept,i will marry you Eddie,you got my word,Antonio whispered,as he and Eddie embraced.

That's what's up! Eddie shouted,his deep voice echoing through the silent room.Damn dude,so you really wanna go through with this? Antonio whispered with a smile.

Hell yea baby boy,are you serious about this? Eddie questioned.Yea,Antonio smiled.We stuck together for life then,Eddie chuckled.Yea,we are,Antonio spoke.Dont be pissed,but i already told your folks,well,our folks now,Eddie whispered.

You told my father? Antonio said with a curious expression.Yea,and your mother,Eddie said very silently.Antonio paused for a second.How did my mother take it? Antonio questioned silently.

She cried,but she still wants to be there for you,and wants you to be happy,which i can do,Eddie whispered as he held Antonio.Your father was cool about it,he already sees me as family,Eddie said silently.

There's a minor problem tho dude,Eddie said nervously.I told everybody that we would be married tomorrow,Eddie chuckled silently,awaiting Antonio's reaction.

Damn! Tomorrow,im not even prepared,Antonio said nervously.How about next week or next month? Antonio questioned.Nah baby,everybody here,even your mother and father are getting along,Eddie whispered.

What if i change my yes into a no,then would you wait until next week? Antonio smiled.Then i'll kick your ass nigga,Eddie chuckled.Yea,sure your right,Antonio murmured sarcastically with a grin.

Kiss me,Eddie whispered to Antonio,his soon to be spouse.Antonio pressed his lips against Eddie's,that ended the conversation.

Eddie and Antonio headed into the other room,where they were greeted by many relatives and friends,even Rick attended.There's my son and my future son in law! Anthony spoke as Antonio and Eddie entered.

Anthony gave Antonio and Eddie bear hugs.

A woman departed from the kitchen,she was Antonio's mother.She slowly walked toward Antonio,her eyes watery.Hey ma,Antonio spoke softly as the woman caressed his hand.Just speak to the boy Joanne,and stop making a scene,Anthony chuckled.

The two of you are something else,i guess like father,like son,Joanne smiled,as she continued to caress Antonio's hand.I'll admit,im not going to sugar coat it,i dont agree with this,but your my son and that boy loves you,i can see it in his eyes,Joanne smiled.

Im a woman,and you then found a good man before i did,Joanne chuckled silently.He is handsome too,Joanne smirked.

You know your wild cousin Jame's then came out the closet at the family reunion,almost gave your aunt Ester a heart attack,Joanne chuckled deeply,wiping the tears from her eyes.Antonio chuckled also.

That boy still crazy,he asked about you too,here is his number,he wanted me to give that to you,Joanne whispered as she handed Antonio a small piece of paper.

Your mama met a new man,he wants to meet you soon,he's on a business trip right now,he's really nice tho,and hopefully not gay,Joanne murmured as she turned her head towards Anthony.Whatever,Anthony smiled,sipping on a glass of vodka.

Im glad that you followed your dreams and didn't let anybody sway you,that's what makes a man,that's what makes any adult,Joanne smiled,holding her tears back.

I heard you part owner and manager at that pool house,Joanne chuckled.You mean bathhouse,Antonio chuckled deeply.

Oh yea,that's right,the AAA bathhouse right? Joanne smiled.

Your father and them A names,he wanted it to be a family business you know,at least half of his dream was accomplished,he finally got you,but he wont get the third part,aint no grand babies coming his way,he wanted his grandson to complete the circle,fill in that extra A,Joanne chuckled.

Have you slept with that Eddie yet? If you are going down on him,make sure he go down too,you know what i mean,Joanne chuckled deeply.

Ma! Antonio chuckled.You ain't got that ding a ling for nothing,and you are your fathers son,im sure it's at least nine or ten inches,Joanne laughed out.Are you drunk ma? Antonio questioned with a smirk.

No,just having fun baby,but mama about to go upstairs and check her makeup,Joanne whispered as she headed up the stairs.Antonio was glowing from the inside,mostly everyone he loved was in that room.

Antonio could feel warm arms tie around his waist.It was Eddie.If we're getting married let's have a little pratice,Eddie chuckled as he guided Antonio into the other room.They had alot of practice that night.

The sun gleamed across Antonio and Eddie's brown skin as they awoke.

It was their big day.You ready to do this? Eddie questioned with a smile.Yea,Antonio answered quickly.Let's get freshened up then,Eddie said silently.Antonio and Eddie quickly freshened up,and got dressed,wearing their most expensive pieces of clothing.

Everyone headed out at the same time,most of Antonio and Eddie's relatives and friends had spent the night.

Antonio and Eddie's union was about to be final,the paperwork was done,now the vows were about to be exchanged.Wood Lake Springs allowed same sex marriages,but it did not appeal to everyone.

Antonio walked down the aisle,his pulse racing,he didn't imagine this day would come so soon.Everyone watched,with wide smiles on their faces.Antonio tugged against his fancy tuxedo,letting his nerves get the best of him.Anthony wrapped his arm around Antonio's shoulders.Let's make this traditional,Anthony chuckled as he escorted Antonio down the aisle.

Eddie's face lit with joy as Antonio got closer.

Eddie pulled Antonio onto the stage,taking Anthony's place.

Take care of my damn son,Anthony whispered with a smile.I got you,he in good hands,very good hands,Eddie spoke silently.Antonio could barely stare into Eddie's eyes,his nerves still shooting through the roof.

Look at me,Eddie demanded silently.I love you Antonio,and i wanna spend the rest of my life with you dude,Eddie whispered,as he and Antonio faced each other.Likewise,Antonio whispered as he and Eddie held hands.

I want you forever,Antonio whispered.You have my heart,my body and soul,in this life and the next,only god knows how much i love you man,Eddie whispered,two tear drops falling from his eyes.

You about to make me wet my suit up dude,Eddie chuckled.

Antonio's eyes began to water.Do you accept my hand Antonio? Eddie questioned.I do,Antonio answered.Do you accept mine in return? Antonio questioned.You know i do,Eddie smiled.Then i pronounce you husband and husband,mate to mate,partner to partner,the preacher smiled.

Eddie pulled a ring from his tux,placing it on Antonio's finger.Antonio then reached into his pocket,placing a ring on Eddie's finger as well.It's not new,but pricey,Antonio smiled.

I dont give a fuck,kiss me,Eddie ordered Antonio.

Antonio and Eddie's lips united.Everyone stood to their feet,clapping as the pair locked lips.Eddie and Antonio kissed for three minutes,everything else fading into the background.

Eddie's mother blew Antonio and Eddie a kiss,knowing they've been attached since their first year of college.She and

Antonio's mother held hands,while tears shot from their eyes,they were tears of joy,watching their sons grow before their eyes.Eddie and Antonio gave every person in the room a gentle smile as their lips untied.

Eddie and Antonio jumped from the stage,heading towards the exit.The rice was thrown as the newlyweds ran toward the door,trying to avoid it.

Antonio was staring Ricky directly in the eyes as he and Eddie exited the building.Congratulations man,Ricky spoke with a slight smile as he examined Antonio.Let's get out of this joint baby,Eddie said calmly,hoping Ricky would realize Antonio was taken.

Thank's,Antonio replied silently,wanting to forget the brief encounter he had with Ricky at the AAA many months ago.I'll be seeing you around Antonio,catch you later,Ricky whispered as he grazed Antonio's arm.

Eddie pushed his lips into Antonio's,hoping Ricky would get the picture.Dude married now,he's going to be kind of tied up,so that later might turn into a long time bro,Eddie said sarcastically,becoming annoyed at Ricky's advances on Antonio.

Ricky gave Eddie an unfriendly glare as he left the scene.

Antonio and Eddie got into the car,waving at their friends and family as they headed off.

Ricky watched the couple takeoff,his face slightly saddened.

Chapter 8

Eddie and Antonio headed home,after enjoying their first couple of hours of marriage.The sun began to set.Antonio and Eddie spotted a black nissan car in the driveway as they approached.

A woman exited the car as soon as they headed up the pathway.

Im Pam,you remember me? Duane's girlfriend said silently,her face emotionless.You have a visitor,she said quietly,unveiling a small baby carrier from the passenger side of the nissan.

Antonio's eyes widened.

The baby carrier didn't cause his surprise,but the small lookalike inside did.Me and Duane made a plan,the day before we came to your bathhouse,in case you ever snitched.I promised Duane i would help him blackmail you,Pam said with a blank expression.

Duane told me that alot of ya'll have sex in those places,so i took the used condom from the trashcan,the one that was in ya'll room,Pam said quietly.

Duane wanted me to claim you raped me,if you ever called the feds on him.He wanted to keep little a in his corner as ammo,but that nigga is becoming dead to me,Pam explained.Broad get the fuck off this property,im not playing,Eddie said with an angered facial expression.This is your baby,im not lying,look at him,Pam explained,giving

Antonio a closer view of the young baby,her eyes watery.

The baby resembled Antonio and Anthony.

The same smooth brown skin,thick dark hair,and the most adorable eyes.Antonio couldn't deny the resemblance.I know what Duane and his friends did to you,i cant trust them around my baby,i cant trust none of ya'll,but you seem like the better choice,ya'll might be gay,but ya'll seem like decent folks,Pam explained.

Duane did cocaine right in front of little a,i cant have my baby around that shit! Pam yelled.It's your choice,either i take my baby to the adoption center,or little a can stay here with ya'll? At least that'll give little a a father,even if it means having two fathers,Pam explained.

Pam was beginning to grow impatient.Why dont you just leave Duane? Antonio questioned angrily.Because i still love him,Duane aint perfect,but it's something about him,i might not be the best mother,but me making this choice is a step in the right direction.

We'll take the baby,Eddie spoke as he reached for the carrier.

You are a trifling person,but this child shouldn't be blamed for that,Eddie explained calmly.

His name is Antwone,but i call him little a,you and your father have A names,so i thought that name would fit him,here's his birth certificate and his formula is in this bag,Pam explained as tears poured from her eyes.Get the fuck outta here! Antonio yelled.

Pam jumped into the car,quickly pulling off,fleeing the area.

Antonio look at this boy,damn he looks like you,this is my son too man,Eddie smiled.Little dude a part of you,so i aint got no choice but to love him,Eddie said with honesty.

Look at him! Eddie chuckled,lowering the carrier towards Antonio.

Get it away from me,Antonio said silently,his facial expression blank.So you are going to be just like that chick that just left baby,Eddie whispered,as tears rushed down his face.

I know that shit hurts,it's too much on you at once,but we can do this,we partners right? Eddie explained.This is our new life,we married and now we got Antwone to join us.You hear that name?

Antwone,your fathers circle is complete nigga,Eddie whispered.

Antonio was speechless,someone made him a father,without his permission.

The baby boy began to cry out.Antonio jumped to his feet instinctively,this was his paternal side kicking in.Eddie pulled the baby out of the carrier,cradling Antwone in his arms as Antonio stared into the babys eyes.

Antonio felt like his freedom had been taken away from him,twice.But Antonio could not resist the baby boy,there were only three other people in the world who made Antonio feel this way,and that was Eddie,his father Anthony,and his mother Joanne,These people were special to him,and baby Antwone was a new member to that list.

We are a family now man,Eddie chuckled as he placed his arm around Antonio,kissing Antwone on the cheek in the process.

Antonio gently smiled as he examined the baby boy.Eddie placed the baby into Antonio's arms,giving Antonio a chance to hold him.This is our son man,Eddie chuckled as he wrapped his arms around Antonio and Antwone.

They entered the house,where Antonio fed baby Antwone a warm bottle.Let me hold little man,Eddie requested as he reached for Antwone.

Antonio surrendered Antwone into Eddie's arms and then headed into the kitchen,calling Anthony,explaining the news.

Anthony and Joanne rushed to the house,after discovering their unexpected grandchild.

Joanne grabbed baby Antwone from Antonio's arms,as soon as she entered.She began to snuggle and kiss the young baby,not giving Anthony a chance to meet his new grandson.

Anthony finally got his chance to hold Antwone,keeping his tears back as he held the child.Go ahead,let them tears out! Joanne commanded Anthony.He cried like a damn baby when you were born Antonio,Joanne chuckled deeply.

You got your wish Anthony,Joanne smiled softly,tears rushing from her eyes as well.So who is this whore,and how did she get her hands on your soldiers Antonio,I thought you were gay? Joanne questioned,not knowing all the facts.

That's not important,but you can thank Eddie for that,Anthony chuckled.The boy needed some type of stimulation,Anthony continued to chuckle.You are still a pervert Anthony,Joanne smirked.

Ya'll better not have this poor baby up in that bathhouse or im going to have a fit,Joanne explained with a smile.

Im putting his name on the place tomorrow,Anthony smirked.No you are not,Joanne explained.This baby is going to grow up and get another kind of career and marry a nice southern girl,with some good values,Joanne explained,already planning the childs life.

You said the same thing about Antonio,remember,you see his husband over there,Anthony smirked with a sinister smile.

That was your fault,that must of been some gay gene he inherited from you,Joanne joked.Nah,maybe your mom,she always been kind of manly,Anthony smirked.You taken it there Anthony,let's talk about your mother,Joanne explained.

Whatever,here we go,Anthony explained as he and Joanne headed up the stairs with the baby,having a silent spat in the process.

Your folks are crazy,Eddie chuckled,while sitting next to Antonio.Can we trust them to babysit? Eddie laughed out.Antonio laughed also as he and Eddie leaned back,holding each other on the sofa.

It was a long day,Antonio and Eddie's eyes shut.

Chapter 9

Antonio opened his eyes,awakening to a tender moment,spotting Anthony and Antwone on the other couch,nestled together,in a deep slumber.

Antonio rose to his feet,tiptoeing into the kitchen,not wanting to wake the two.Antonio's eyes examined the house,not seeing Eddie anywhere in sight.Antonio prepared a bottle for baby Antwone and then crept back towards the couch,where his father and son slept silently.

Antonio reached for Antwone,but was alarmed by loud voices,coming from outside.The voices got louder,but not loud enough to wake Anthony and the baby.This wasn't a conversation,but an argument.

Antonio headed towards the sound,slightly pulling the curtains back.Antonio spotted a car in the driveway,it was the same black nissan from earlier.The same car Duane's girlfriend Pam drove.

Antonio saw Eddie in a heated argument with someone,but could not fully see the persons face.

There were three people in total,Eddie and the two people who he argued with.Antonio quietly opened the front door,heading into the yard.There were only a few residents in the area,so no one bothered to complain about the noise,because only a few lived there,and their houses were seperated by tall trees.

Antonio headed towards the group.

What's going on? Antonio questioned silently.Antonio now saw who the other two were,it was Pam and Duane.What are you doing here? Antonio questioned with a slight frown.We are here to take little man home,that's why we here,Duane answered angrily.

Duane calm down baby,im going to find a way to get him back,i promise,just cool down,Pam explained timidly.

Cool down?! We wouldn't be in this predicament,if your stupid ass wouldn't have brung the little nigga here! Duane yelled.That was my fault,but let me handle this,Pam explained.

Antonio can i have my baby back? I shouldn't have dropped him on you like that,that was wrong of me,im pretty sure you got alot on your plate,but im here to bring him home,Pam explained calmly.

Leave this fucking area,and dont come back! Eddie shouted to Duane and Pam.

Nah,we aint leaving until ya'll bring little a out this motherfucker,Duane spoke.Nigga you dont give a fuck about that little boy,you just want to use him,in case we report your bitch ass,Eddie explained.

Look,just bring the little dude out here,and it wont be no trouble,Duane said.

She left him with us,and that's where he's staying,Antonio spoke.That's her motherfucking baby,if she wants to take him back,she can do that,Duane spoke,his patients running thin.Can i have him back? Pam said quietly,not wanting the situation to get out of hand.

No,do you want me to repeat it,Antonio said angrily.

Fuck that! Report their asses,Duane explained.Report?! Nigga you go right ahead,because it's alot of shit we can report,Eddie frowned.So are you bringing up old shit? Duane questioned.You damn right,Eddie explained himself.

The shit aint that old and secondly,the shit was a crime,Eddie spoke silently.You lucky your ass aint in the penitentiary,Eddie spoke as he gave Duane a nasty stare.

You going to get yours homey,Duane replied as he pulled Pam by the arm,heading towards the car.

Get the fuck in the car! Duane ordered Pam as he got into the driver seat.You are a dumb bitch man,you then gave them niggas more power,Duane complained.Duane could no longer argue with Antonio and Eddie,knowing he had plenty of skeletons in his closet.

Duane pulled off,the tires screeching against the ground as he and Pam hit the open road.

I cant believe the nerve of those two motherfuckers,Eddie explained.You telling me,Antonio exhaled in agreement.

Eddie and Antonio headed back into the house,after their disagreement with Duane and Pam.

Im going to take little man to the room and feed him,Eddie explained as he gently grabbed little a from Anthony's arms.He can stay with me,Anthony explained with weary eyes,still tired.

No pops,you get your sleep,Antonio explained silently.Antonio watched Eddie feed Antwone,admiring the sight.I can take it fron here Eddie,Antonio whispered as he reached for little a.

Eddie was very good with baby Antwone,as if he had pratice.

Eddie headed into the other room,shutting the door silently as he departed the room.Antonio used this quiet time to bond even more with his son.Antonio heard a quiet knock at his bedroom door.Come in,Antonio answered.

It was Joanne,she had left the house,without anyone knowing.She wasn't alone,she pushed in an expensive baby crib.I cant let my first grandchild go without a bed,she laughed out.Thank's ma,Antonio chuckled.No problem baby,Joanne whispered as she gave Antwone a quick peck on the cheek.

I'll leave you two alone,Joanne smiled as she exited the room.

Antonio held little a in his arms,until the baby boy finally fell asleep.Antonio placed Antwone into the crib,and then headed into the other room,keeping his room door open.Antonio and Eddie cuddled on the sofa,and then fell asleep.

It was the next day.

Everyone awoke to the crying baby,that started the day.Antonio and Eddie headed out that morning,bringing Antwone with them.Antonio didn't just buy things for himself,but the baby also.Antonio had brought the baby an entire wardrobe and a list of baby items.

Antonio and Eddie and little a had spent almost the entire day out,but soon headed home.

Antonio and Eddie unloaded the car,and then took little a and the items inside.Antonio set little a in his crib,and then headed back into the other room,helping Eddie unpack,keeping the bedroom door open,in case little a cried out.

Antonio could hear footsteps traveling down the stairs.

Two women entered the kitchen.One of those women were Antonio's mother and the other was an uninvited guest.The other woman was Pam,Duane's girlfriend and the mother of baby Antwone.Antonio and Eddie's eyes widened as they examined Pam's face.

Pam's face was covered in bruises.Pam's left eye was puffy and unable to fully open.Pam's bottom lip had two visible cuts across it,and her face appeared swollen.

The bruises gave Pam's usual light brown complexion a reddish blue tone,mostly around her eyes and cheeks.

What are you doing here,again? Antonio questioned Pam silently,still examining her bruises.

And what happened to your face? Antonio whispered.That motherfucking Duane then beat her ass,Eddie explained with a smirk.Duane raised his hand to me,Pam whispered,blood still staining her lips.

Duane had released his fury on pam,still angry about the other day.

Im about to go upstairs,and give ya'll some privacy,Joanne murmured silently,gently grazing Pam's shoulders as she headed upstairs,feeling sorry for the woman.

I dont mean to laugh baby girl,but what do you expect from a dude like Duane? Eddie explained.

Im gone for good this time,Duane hit the wrong bitch,Pam spoke with anger in her eyes.Im going to get him fucked up,you just watch,Pam spoke angrily,holding her swollen and pain filled face.

I know i fucked ya'll over,but can i stay here with ya'll? Pam questioned silently.You made a poor choice in men and now you want us to pay for the consequences? Antonio spoke.

I am so sorry,for everything,but i have nowhere else to go,Pam cried out.And you want us to let you stay here,after all the shit you and your wack ass boyfriend put my dude and me through? Eddie spoke with a serious expression.

That's water under the bridge,im through with his ass,Pam explained.

You did some dirty shit,but you are Antwone's mother,and who knows,you might be lying about that,Antonio said quietly.You can stay,but only if it's ok with Ed,Antonio spoke.Ed? Pam questioned.Short for Eddie,you know who im talking about,Antonio spoke.

Oh,Pam answered in a silent muffle,holding her jaw.

We married now,so i gotta check with you too,Antonio murmured to Eddie.It's cool with me,but i cant fully trust her ass,Eddie explained.To seal the deal,we getting a dna test tomorrow,Antonio spoke silently.You think little a isn't yours? Pam questioned.

Nah,i just wanna make sure you are who you say you are,Antonio explained.

Antonio was indeed Antwone's biological father,but he did not trust Pam.The next morning Antonio and Pam,including little a headed to the local hospital,where they had a dna test done.A week had passed.The dna test results were sent through the mail.

The results were positive,Antonio was Antwone's biological father,and Pam was Antwone's real mother.Antonio's curiosity was cured.

Antonio also got an hiv test done,knowing he was molested by Duane and his friends without any protection.Antonio did not know his status,but he was about to find out.The hiv test came back negative,Antonio was clean.

Antonio changed Antwone's last name,giving Antwone his families last name.

Antwone was now Antwone Neilson.Antonio also asked his father if Pam could stay,even tho he owned his side of the house,which was equipped with everything a condo would consist of.

Antonio had the section remodeled,making space for the baby.Antonio would eventually move out,he and his growing family,but

Anthony suggested he stay another two years.

Antonio listened to his fathers words,and decided to stay,but not for two years,only a couple of months.

Chapter 10

Five months had passed.

It was a saturday night.Antonio and Eddie placed baby rattles above baby Antwone's head,dangling them back and forth as Antwone giggled.

Pam watched from the other room,becoming envious of the sight,wishing that were her and Duane and the baby playing house,instead of them.Pam entered the room,snatching little a from his crib,letting her envy take control.

A child aint supposed to have two daddies,i know ya'll used to this lifestyle,but bring it to a minimum when ya'll around my baby,Pam ordered with a slight frown.Your baby? You know you didn't make that baby alone right? Antonio frowned.

I know that,but have ya'll read the bible yet? What ya'll doing aint right,Pam explained.Oh,so your a saint? Antonio spoke sarcastically.I didn't say that,but im just saying,Pam whispered.

Antonio began to quote verses from the bible,verses that made Pam feel guilty,stopping her in her tracks.

Im over this,look,im about to give Antwone his bath,i'll bring him back,once im done,Pam explained silently.Pam headed into the bathroom,running baby Antwone a bubble bath,and then gently pulled his baby sleeper from his tiny body.

Pam then placed baby Antwone into the warm water,not taking the time to check the water temperature.Antwone giggled as she began to wash him.

Antonio and Eddie sat in the other room,they were alone,they used this alone time to their advantage.Eddie unbuttoned Antonio's shirt,and then slid Antonio's pants and underwear to the floor.Antonio began to discard Eddie's clothes as well.They both were soon completely naked,although Eddie still wore his socks.

Eddie towered over Antonio,he and Antonio were united,their lips meeting.

Antonio and Eddie began their sexual activities,forgetting to completely close the door.

Pam let the water out of the tub,as she scooped up Antwone.You like the water,dont you? She murmured to baby Antwone as she placed a towel around him,covering his entire body,except his head,not wanting him to catch a cold.

Pam was about to enter the room,but was alarmed by Eddie and Antonio's low moans.She peeped through the slightly opened crack of the door,witnessing Antonio and Eddie's steamy love making.

Pam's eyes widened.Pam decided to go into the other room,not wanting to intrude on the pair.

Pam spotted Anthony in the hallway,exiting from the bathroom.Im sorry,Pam whispered,seeing that Anthony had just finished bathing also,wearing nothing but a towel.

Do you mind watching him for me? Pam explained silently.Yea,that's my grandson,give him here,Anthony said without hesitation.Pam gently placed baby Antwone in Anthony's arms,and then headed into the bathroom.

You coming with granddaddy,Anthony chuckled as he carried Antwone into his room,turning on the kids network for Antwone as he dried himself and Antwone off.

Pam filled the sink with water,and then splashed a handful of water on her face.She then headed back into the other section of the house,quietly peeping in on Antonio and Eddie as they made love.

Pam placed two of her fingers in her mouth,getting them wet,and then eased her fingers towards her crouch.Pam tucked her hand into her pants,playing with her female parts as she watched the men in action.

Pam's loins heated,as she went deeper into her flesh.Antonio and Eddie finished before she could,quickly washing themselves off,in the other bathroom,placing their clothes on again.

Pam's live adult film was cut short,and her pleasure was short lived.

Pam quickly headed into the other bathroom,washing her hands,slightly readjusting her pants.

Pam headed to Anthony's room,about to pickup Antwone,but decided to let him stay with Anthony,seeing them enjoying the tv together.Antonio and Eddie headed into the kitchen,they had the munchies.

Pam gave Antonio and Eddie a quick glance,before sitting at the table.

What's wrong with you? Eddie questioned Pam.Nothing,but i saw ya'll getting busy,Pam murmured silently.Oh damn! Eddie responded,not knowing he and Antonio had an audience.Damn,i thought you was giving Antwone a bath? Antonio spoke quietly.

Yea,but it takes no time to wash him,he is a baby,Pam explained.

Hold on,where he at?! Antonio spoke,his face worried.He with your father,he alright,Pam explained.Oh,Antonio exhaled,thinking Pam might have left Antwone alone in the bathtub.

Im not that bad of a mother,Pam smirked.

Anthony headed out of his room,holding baby Antwone in his arms,they were fully dressed in matching outfits.What the hell? Antonio questioned.I did the same thing with you Antonio,so dont act brand new,Anthony chuckled.

We about to hit the town fair,they got kid friendly activities as well as adult ones,Anthony explained.That's today? Antonio spoke silently.Yep,it started around six pm,it doesn't end until twelve am,ya'll wanna come? Anthony questioned.

I'll go,Eddie spoke.Me too,Antonio agreed.I guess i'll come too,Pam whispered.Everyone headed out that night,enjoying themselves at the town fair.

The town fair was a special event for the small town.Antonio and Eddie participated in activities,while Anthony showed off his grandson.Pam walked around,watching,but not participating in the activities.

Pam lit a cigarette and then headed behind a tree to smoke it.

Pam wasn't the only one there,Duane was also behind the tree,receiving oral sex from a blue eyed caucasian male.

Damn,what the fuck you doing here? Duane whispered.Pam spit her cigarette from her mouth,and then began to cry,running in the other direction.Pam! Wait man,Duane ordered,pushing the man from his hardened genitals.

Duane pulled his pants up and then quickly followed behind Pam.

Duane caught Pam,before she could enter the crowd.

Duane took Pam behind a tree,shoving her against it.Duane began to scold her,as if she were a child.I heard you was living with them niggas,Duane spoke angrily.And if i was? Pam replied with an attitude.

I know you miss me,bring your ass home,Duane spoke silently,pushing himself closer to Pam.

So you can beat my ass again? Pam said through her teeth.You pretend like i dont know the things you do,Pam whispered.Whatever,it's just sex,Duane answered quietly.It's not just sex,it's the drugs and the beatings,and you shoving your dick in anything,Pam explained.

I love you Pam,just come home,Duane said as he rested his head on Pam's shoulder.You'll never change,Pam explained as she pushed Duane from her.Pam then spit in Duane's face.

Duane wiped his face with his shirt and then raised his fist,about to hit Pam,but instead reached into his pants pocket,pulling out a small pistol.

Duane waved the pistol in Pam's face,trying to intimidate her.

Pam began to silently cry.Bring your ass back home,you and the boy,Duane ordered,as he released Pam from his grip.Pam ran into the crowd again,hiding her emotions.

It was soon time to go,everyone headed home.Antonio reached for Antwone,gently removing him from Anthony's arms.Everyone was tired.Antonio placed baby Antwone into his crib,where Antwone slept through the night and so did everyone else.

Pam cried that whole night,before falling asleep,but her tears faded,Pam knew she had evidence of a petty crime Duane had once committed.

The next morning Pam had Duane arrested.Duane was sentenced to two years in prison.

Chapter 11

Five years had passed.

Duane had served his two year prison sentence,and spent the other three years getting back on his feet.Duane knew who was responsible for his arrest,but it was only a matter of time,before he confronted the person.

A lot of things had changed during those five years,baby Antwone was growing,now able to speak fluently.Antwone could almost outrun Antonio,but he still had a lot of growing up to do,and Antonio and the rest of his family would be there with him.

Baby Antwone was spoiled by Antonio and Anthony,including Eddie,but Pam didn't agree with that,thinking he might turnout the wrong way.Pam thought Antwone would become selfish and spoiled.

But Pam also thought Antwone would grow up to be gay,him being spoiled and sheltered by the three men in his life.

Antonio and Anthony,including Eddie proved to Pam that not all men were the same,and also changed her view on gay men as well.Antonio decided to stay another five years,raising little a in the same house he grew up in,and also maintaining his strong marriage with Eddie.

Can we go to the park? Antwone questioned in his small child voice.

Yea,Antonio answered as he pat Antwone on the head.Antonio gave little a another stare,wondering how he could have been so emotionless about the boys existence,the first day he discovered Antwone was his son.

Antonio's feelings for Antwone had grown beyond his imagination,a father and son bond,but they were also friends.

Antwone placed his finished homework in a pile on the table,getting prepared for a day at the park.Antwone was very smart and well mannered,and could pass for a mini duplicate of Antonio,and his grandfather Anthony.

There were small traces of Pam in Antwone as well.Antwone may not have been blood related to Eddie,but shared a deep and loving relationship with him,Eddie was another father figure to Antwone.

Antwone and his mother got along well,but there was something still bothering Pam,somethhing she yearned for.

Duane was doing well,no one knew what he did to make a living,but he did it well,Pam had learned this,and thought maybe Duane had finally changed his ways.

Antonio placed little a on the couch,tickling Little a's stomach.

Antwone giggled as Antonio tickled him.Alright,go put on your shoes,Antonio spoke to Antwone.Eddie helped Antwone put on his shoes,and then performed a secret handshake with him.Antonio grabbed Antwone's arm as they headed out the door,assisting him.

Antonio and Antwone spent almost the entire day at the park,leaving once it became dark out.

The next day came in a flash.Antonio woke up,about to help Antwone prepare for school,but Pam beat him to the punch.Pam packed Antwone's backpack,packing it with more than it could handle.

Pam impatiently paced back and forth,nervously getting herself prepared also.I'll take little a to school today,Pam explained to Antonio.Are you sure? I mean,i have no problem taking him,Antonio spoke silently.You seem out of it,Antonio said silently,watching the sweat drip from Pam's neck.

Im cool,i gotta stop pass the grocery store anyway,Pam explained nervously,trying to put on a straight face.

Alright,but i'll pick Antwone up this afternoon,Antonio spoke as he kneeled down,giving Antwone a quick peck on the forehead.See you later on little man,Eddie waved to Antwone.See you later daddy and Eddie,Antwone smiled.

Go tell your grandfather goodbye,Pam whispered to Antwone.

Antwone headed into his Grandfathers room,leaping on his bed,awakening Anthony from his slumber.See you grandpa,Antwone chuckled as he and Anthony playfully wrestled.Alright baby boy,have fun at school,and i'll see you later,Anthony spoke to Antwone.

Anthony gave Antwone a big hug,and then allowed him to get back to his destination,which was school.

Antwone gave his family another goodbye wave,before he and his mother departed from the house,that was the last time Antwone was heard or seen by his family,the last time he would wave his family goodbye.

Pam was also nowhere to be found.

Antonio spoke with Antwone's school teacher and other staff members,questioning them about Antwone's disappearance,no one saw Antwone,saying that he never came to school that day.

Antwone's absence caused Antonio and Eddie and Anthony to worry,not seeing the young boy since morning.Antonio texted Pam repeatly,but she never responded back to them,this made

Antonio go into a deep depression,not
hearing or seeing his son,not having a
clue where he was,not knowing if he was
with Pam or somewhere else,not
knowing if he still had air in his lungs or
if he was in danger.

Chapter 12

Little a and Pam were missing for
weeks,the weeks turned into months
and the months turned into years.

Pam had secretly reunited with Duane,and began living with him,her and little a.

Pam became pregnant,in her third year of living with Duane,the unborn child Pam carried inside of her was Duane's,but to Duane it didn't matter,he forced Pam to have an abortion,but married her afterwards,thinking that would make up for his behavior.

Fifteen years had passed since little a and Pam went missing.

Antonio and Eddie were no longer twenty somethings,but in their mid thirties,still being able to pass for twenty five year olds.

Antwone was no longer little a,but big A.

Antwone was now twenty years old.

Chapter 13

Antwone headed out the bathroom,he had just finished showering.Antwone draped a towel around his waist as he headed to his room.Antwone heard a whistle,he turned towards the sound,spotting his stepfather Duane sitting on the couch,with his legs open,holding a remote.

Come here Antwone,Duane whispered.Antwone nervously headed towards Duane.Sit down,Duane ordered silently,wanting Antwone to join him on the couch.Duane switched the tv off and then placed the remote on the side of the couch.

Where your moms? Duane questioned Antwone.

She left out,i just gave her money to pay the gas bill,Antwone spoke silently in his adult voice,not wanting to sit next to Duane.What are you getting fresh for?

Where are you about to go? Duane questioned Antwone.

Nowhere,i just needed to shower,and im not finished,Antwone spoke softly.Yea,i can see that,get over here,Duane said silently as he moved Antwone closer.

Not today man,Antwone spoke,his face annoyed.Sit in my lap nigga,Duane commanded.Duane gapped his legs open even further,wearing a pair of blue denim jeans,and a black t shirt.

Antwone gently sat in Duane's lap and then began to move in a circular motion,pushing himself back onto Duane,Duane bit the edge of his lip,enjoying it.Duane grabbed Antwone's waist,pushing him down faster.

Duane didn't bother to pull his pants down or unwrap Antwone's towel,but continued the motion.Antwone could feel Duane's hardened rod rubbing against his backside,but wanted it to be over quickly.

Duane moaned out,spilling himself inside of his jeans and underwear.

Im done,go ahead and finish doing what you was doing,Duane ordered Antwone,catching his breath in the process.This wasn't the first time Duane put Antwone in this position,it started once Antwone turned eighteen.

Antwone didn't like the things he did with Duane,but did it anyway,knowing if he didn't Duane would find some reason to start a big fight with his mother Pam.

Antwone was becoming tired of it all,secretly searching for an apartment,somewhere he and his mother could stay,far away from Duane.

Antwone headed into his room,leaping into his bed,wanting to forget everything,while Duane switched the tv back on.

The hours passed as Antwone slept silently and naked on his bed,after taking two benadryl pills.Antwone headed into the bathroom,wanting to take another shower,feeling dirty,after his situation with Duane.

It was dark out,but the house was lit by dim lights.

Antwone washed himself up again,and then headed back into the living room,wrapping his towel around his waist.Antwone spotted his mother in the corner,doing cocaine,but she tried to conceal it,once she spotted Antwone as well.

Ma! Are you okay? Antwone questioned.

Im fine baby,just go finish drying off,Pam stuttered,her speech affected by the drugs.Pam looked older than her actual age.Antwone headed into the kitchen,about to brew Pam a cup of tea,hoping that would awaken her senses.

The gas ain't working.Ma did you pay the gas company? Antwone murmured.Yea,Pam said repeatedly.Pam was lying,she had used the money to buy cocaine for herself and Duane.

Antwone's face became saddened,as he watched his mother struggle with her addiction.Duane headed into the living room,just entering the house.Pam you better not had used all of that shit! Duane shouted.

Why is this boy always naked? Duane spoke,examining Antwone's half naked body.Do you see the way this boy walk around? That's disrespectful Pam,Duane explained.

Pam headed into the room,ignoring Duane.Antwone sat on the couch,watching the tv.

Duane went into the bathroom,bathing himself for ten minutes and then headed back into the living room,wrapping a towel around his waist,joining Antwone on the couch.

Antwone adjusted his towel,moving to the other side of the couch.

Why you not in the other room with my mother? Antwone questioned silently.Your moms is high,and i wanna watch the game,Duane explained.Give me the remote,Duane ordered Antwone.

I was watching the tv first,Antwone said quietly.

I dont give a damn,Duane frowned as he snatched the remote from Antwone's hand.If you want it back,reach for it nigga,Duane whispered as he tucked the remote in his towel.

Antwone frowned,letting Duane have his way.

Pam was in a deep sleep,not hearing anything.Nah,im just playing with you little dude,heres the remote,Duane smirked as he pulled his equipment from the slit in his towel.

Come in get it,Duane chuckled.

That's nasty man,Antwone frowned,feeling uncomfortable.Antwone rose from the couch,about to head into his room,but was grabbed by Duane.Where you going? Stay here and watch the game,you dont like football or something? Duane questioned silently.

Nah,i just want to get out of this towel and put on some clothes,Antwone explained.I was just fooling around with you,sit back down,Duane ordered silently.

Duane quickly placed Antwone's hand around his stiff manhood as Antwone sat back down.I dont wanna do this,my mother,your wife is in the other room,Antwone explained eagerly.She probably sleep,jerk that shit,Duane ordered Antwone.

Antwone squeezed Duane's hardened man part,hoping Duane would feel pain,but Duane enjoyed it.You think that shit hurt nigga? Duane smirked.You are just going to make me cum quicker,Duane smiled and then began to moan.

You are fucking trifling,does my mother know that you fuck other women and men? Antwone spoke silently.And now your trying to get with me,Antwone frowned.It's none of your moms business,Duane murmured.

That's your wife dude,that is her business,Antwone explained.

Stop mouthing off at me Antwone,Duane said quietly.Open your mouth and get on your knees,since you wanna keep mouthing off little nigga,Duane commanded.

Duane gently placed Antwone's mouth on the tip of his manhood,and then began to push Antwone's head up and down.Im going to tell my mother man,Antwone spoke,muffled by Duane's equipment,tears pouring down his eyes.You aint going to tell nobody,now shut up and keep sucking that shit,Duane ordered in a moan.

You look just like your father nigga,he was a queer ass nigga,just like you,Duane moaned as he continued to force himself into Antwone's mouth.

You just giving me head,you better hope i dont fuck you too,Duane explained silently.Keep on crying nigga,you are going to make me cum in your fucking mouth,Duane loudly moaned out,feeling himself about to explode.

Use some tongue nigga,suck stepdaddy dick,Duane moaned,as Antwone gulped and swallowed his man part.

Duane pulled Antwone from his rod,feeling pity for Antwone,not wanting to release himself in Antwone's mouth,but kissed Antwone on the lips instead,gently sliding his tongue into Antwone's mouth,shooting his thick manhood substance onto Antwone's pecks.

Duane dried himself with his towel as he released his lips from Antwone's.Bitch ass nigga,go in the room and clean yourself off,Duane ordered Antwone.

If you Tell your mother,watch me get up in your ass the next time,Duane exhaled as Antwone headed to his room,ripping his towel from his waist as he fled Duane's sight.

Chapter 14

Antwone went into his room,and then began to lay on his side,his body curled up,fully nude.

Duane headed in a few minutes afterwards,gently positioning himself beside Antwone,he was fully nude himself,no longer covered with his towel.Get the fuck out my bed dude! Antwone yelled.

Make me nigga,Duane whispered.

Duane stared into Antwone's eyes,mesmerized by Antwone's sex appeal.Antwone closed his eyes,not wanting to stare Duane in the eyes.I remember when you was just a little nigga,now you grown,Duane whispered.Do you love me nigga? Tell me the truth,i never abused you or nothing like that,and a boy needs a man in his life,Duane spoke silently.

Answer me nigga? Duane said,awaiting Antwone's response.

Yea,i did,at one point in time,but once that sex shit started you kind of threw me off man,Antwone explained silently.Nigga you aint no kid no more,people are going to look at you diffrently,as you got older i became attracted to you nigga,i shouldn't be feeling that way about you,but you aint my real son,Duane whispered.

But you're my stepdad dude,your supposed to be another parent to me Duane,Antonio whispered,tears rolling down his eyes.

Duane paused,after listening to Antwone's speech.Dude what happened to you? What made you turnout like this? Antwone questioned Duane.What the fuck you mean by that? Duane spoke with anger.

Did you get abused or something? Antwone murmured.

My father caught me jacking off to gay porn when i was sixteen,nigga beat the shit outta me,he fucked me up with his fist and a baseball bat,i had to be rushed to the hospital,i had internal bleeding,my moms just sat there,he ended up beating her ass too,thinking she was responsible.

Where he at now? Antwone questioned silently.Nigga was killed in prison,nigga didn't want to be nobodies bitch and he didn't want to convert to muslim or join a group,in prison you gotta choose,Duane whispered.

Antwone became silent,turning over on his other side.Antwone's naked backside grazed Duane's exposed prick.Antwone became nervous,forgetting Duane was behind him.

Duane's prick became erect,feeling the naked flesh of Antwone's behind.

You like teasing me dont you? Duane whispered,his breath beating against Antwone's neck.Man i wasn't trying to tease you,i did that shit by accident,Antwone explained.

Duane pushed his head towards Antwone's neck,placing his right thigh towards Antwone's,climbing on top of Antwone,his crotch towards Antwone's behind.Duane pulled his arms towards each side of Antwone.

The position would be considered scandalous,for some viewers,Duane and Antwone being stepfather and stepson.

Pam entered the room,seeing Duane and Antwone in their state,her blood boiled,as she witnessed the naked pair tightly snuggled together.Ma wait! Antwone shouted.Duane quickly moved himself away from Antwone,after Pam walked in.

Pam ran into the other room,and then reentered with a pistol.

What the fuck was you doing to my baby Duane?! Pam shouted,her eyes red and watery as she pointed the gun in Duane's direction.The veins in Pam's eyes were very visible,caused by anger and drugs.

Pam's anger and the drugs made a bad combination.

Duane was clueless,not knowing that Pam knew exactly where he hid his gun.

Put it down Pam,Duane whispered in fear.Im going to ask you again,what the fuck was you doing to my motherfucking child?! Pam screamed.

It's okay ma,im fine,Antwone spoke nervously.Im about to pack my shit and leave,Duane explained quietly,not wanting to upset Pam any further.You see him as a piece of ass now huh,Pam murmured,her hands shaking.

Pam pulled the trigger.

One bullet exited the gun,intended for Duane.The bullet grazed Duane's neck,leaving a tiny scrape and blood.Duane flinched,feeling the heat from the bullet that almost killed him.

Duane quickly ran from the room,but was followed by Pam.

Chapter 15

Pam pulled the trigger three more times,missing Duane with every shot.Pam being high was the cause of her missing Duane.Duane locked himself into the other room,quickly placing his clothes on.

Im sorry Pam! Duane shouted.

Antwone gently removed the gun from his mothers hand,hugging her in the process.Antwone and Pam cried as they hugged.Duane quickly ran out of the house,seeing Pam preoccupied.

This is my fault baby,Pam cried as she held Antwone in her arms.

No it's not,just rest ma,Antwone whispered as he escorted his mother to the bedroom,placing her on the bed.Antwone slept beside his mother.

Antwone awoke,seeing his mother still asleep.

Antwone tiptoed into his room,about to place on fresh clothes,but was distracted by a new sight.His entire stash of benadryl was opened.Antwone's thoughts began to wander,he then quickly ran into the other room,where his mother slept.

Pam was still asleep,but this wasn't normal slumber,this slumber was caused by an overdose.Pam was extremely distraught after the situation with Duane,thinking drugs and more drugs was the only answer,even using household medical drugs to lift her pain.

Pam had took almost the entire stash of Antwone's benadryl.Antwone blamed himself.Antwone quickly called for an ambulance as he swiftly placed on his clothes.Pam was rushed to the hospital,choking and gagging along the way as she was revived.

You ok ma? Antwone spoke to his mother as she laid in the hospital bed.

Im fine baby,just be strong,Pam whispered.I love you Antwone and im so sorry for any harm i caused you,Pam explained.It's ok ma,Antwone whispered as he held onto his mothers thin and frail hand.

I kept you away from your father and your other family,hoping i could start one with you me and Duane,but please dont hold that against me baby,Pam begged for forgiveness.

I wont,you're still my mother,Antwone spoke silently as tears rushed from his eyes,soaking his clothes.

They all loved you,your father,your other stepfather and your grandfather,but i was stupid,stupid for ripping you away from them,Pam murmured silently.I didn't think that Duane would make a move on you,but i should've known,after what happened to your father,Pam explained.

What happened to my father? Antonio questioned,his face confused.

Before you were born your father was sexually assaulted by Duane and a few of Duane's friends,Pam explained silently.Why aren't they locked up? Antwone questioned.

Your father had a soft heart,but Duane and his friends got the shit beat out of them,especially Duane,he got a ass whooping from your father and another ass whooping after that,your grandfather aint no joke,none of the Neilson men are,Pam coughed.

I thought Duane had changed,but he remained the same,Pam spoke silently.I want you to go home and get some sleep and then search through my dresser,you should find a blue safe,that's yours,Pam whispered to Antwone.

Your father was building you a trust fund,but i stole it,the same day i took you away,Pam said,guilt fuming from her face.

I never spent a dime of it,i even threw away the key,in case i got tempted,Pam explained.You'll figure out a way to open it,Pam grinned,her eyes tired and weary.

Go home baby,your mother is a fighter,i'll be okay,Pam whispered.

Antwone gave his mother a kiss on the cheek and then headed home.

Antwone fell asleep in his bed that night,the house was quiet and empty with the exception of Antwone.Antwone woke up the next morning,brushing his teeth and then taking a quick shower.

Antwone placed his clothes on and then began to search his mothers dresser,finding the blue safe,buried under clothes.

Antwone examined the safe as he held it in his hands,not knowing how to open it.Antwone quickly tucked the safe under his bed,hearing someone enter the house,he and Pam and Duane were the only ones who had keys.

Antwone peeped around the corner,spotting Duane and two other men.

Antwone's heart jumped,as he witnessed the trio roam the

house.Antwone silently shut his door,hoping no one knew he was there.Come out Antwone,i know you here,i saw your moms being carried away in the ambulance and your keys on the table,Duane said in a clear voice.

Antwone entered the living room,stepping into full view of Duane and the others.

Damn! Dude look just like his pops,one of the men explained as he examined Antwone.You aint lying Markus,the other man chuckled in agreement.The men were Markus and Jim,the same men who helped Duane sexually assault

Antwone's father Antonio a long time ago.

Markus and Jim were older now,including Duane,but still maintained their good looks,their good looks wasn't the only thing they maintained,they were still up to no good.

Chapter 16

Look at them lips,his father had the same lips,Markus explained to Jim with a smirk.

Jim headed towards Antonio,sipping on a can of beer.Nice seeing you,you probably dont know me,but Duane talks about you all the time,and i saw you once or twice when you was a kid,Jim spoke,his eyes studying Antwone's body.

You built like your father,ya'll Neilson men got some nice bodies,Jim chuckled,lust filling his thoughts as he continued to examine Antwone's figure.

You got a girlfriend? Markus questioned Antwone.Nah,too busy for one of those,Antwone answered nervously.What about a boyfriend then? Jim smirked.That's kind of personal,Antwone whispered.Cool by me youngster,Jim murmured silently.

Leave the dude alone! Duane shouted to his friends.

Tell your mother i got all of my shit,im staying at Markus's place Antwone,Duane explained.Alright,Antwone responded.We outta here,Duane said as he headed towards the door.

Jim purposely brushed his prick against Antwone's arm as he headed towards the door also,giving Antwone a smile.Markus whispered something into Duane's ear,before they could exit the house.Duane and Markus whispered for two minutes and then watched Antwone out of the corner of their eyes.

Markus then whispered to Jim.

Jim smiled in response.You ever tried this shit? Markus questioned Antwone as he pulled a bag of cocaine from his pants pocket.No,not my thing,Antwone answered politely,hoping the men left out.

Try it and see if you like it,Jim explained.Can i stay for a few hours? Duane questioned Antwone.I dont think my mother would be cool with it,but i guess so,Antwone replied,not really wanting Duane or the other two men to stay.

Antwone didn't want to cause any commotion,so he let the men stay.

Markus and Jim sandwiched Antwone on the couch,smoking and sniffing,while Antwone watched.

Loosen up Antwone,these niggas cool,Duane explained as he sniffed cocaine from his wrist.Duane and his friends stayed longer than Antwone expected.Markus offered Antwone cocaine again,placing it on his palm.Try it dude,you'll like it,Markus insisted.

Im cool,no thanks,Antwone said quietly.

Markus rushed his palm into Antwone's nose,trying to force Antwone to sniff the cocaine.If you dont sniff it you aint going to be able to breathe,Markus grinned.Antwone inhaled the cocaine and then began to choke.

Markus and Jim began to laugh.Jim placed something in a cup of beer,handing the cup to Antwone.This will make you feel even better,Jim whispered to Antwone as he placed the cup to Antwone's lips.Antwone swallowed half of the spiked beer down his throat,hoping they would leave after they got him high.Antwone underestimated the tactics of Duane and his group.Ten minutes passed.

Antwone struggled to keep himself conscious,feeling an intense heat throughout his body.

Antwone began to laugh at all of Duane and his gangs jokes,even if they weren't that funny.This boy high as a motherfucker,Markus chuckled.Duane and the others were more capable of handling themselves under the influence of drugs,because they were used to it,unlike Antwone.

Get him out of them clothes,Markus whispered to Jim.

Jim didn't hesitate,that was something he was looking forward to.Jim slid his hand underneath Antwone's shirt,pulling it off.He then gently pulled down Antwone's pants and underwear.

Antwone was fully naked.

Jim began to suck on Antwone's pecks,unzipping his pants,stroking himself as he continued to suck on Antwone's chest.Markus began to take off his clothes,and so did Duane.

Jim then began to fully undress,gently massaging Antwone's abs.

Markus headed towards Antwone,sucking on the back of

antwone's ear,while Duane reached for his cell phone.Duane made a quick call,and then joined in with the activities.Damn! This nigga smooth and toned,Markus whispered,lusting after Antwone's body.

I told you,little dude is fine as fuck,Duane said with conviction.

Antwone became slightly aware of the situation,but was still dazed and confused.

Antwone gently pushed Jim away.Dont be pushing me away nigga,Jim whispered,continuing with his sexual advances on Antwone.Jim then shoved his tongue into Antwone's mouth,pushing his prick against Antwone's leg.

Markus wrapped his arms around Antwone's waist,rubbing his hardened prick onto Antwone's back.

The room was warm,heated by the hot naked bodies.

Duane was about to kiss Antwone,but was disturbed by a silent noise,Someone was at the door,knocking silently.Duane headed towards the door,peeping out of the peephole and then opening the door.

Duane let the stranger in,it was a tall female.

The woman entered the house,she wore nothing but a long leather coat and a pair of high heels,her hair cut short,she was the age of twenty three.I need my money upfront,the young woman demanded.

You'll get it once were fucking done,Duane whispered.

Whatever,just make this shit quick,the woman said as she pulled her coat from her naked body,joining the group.

Jim began to suck on the womans breast,but continued to massage

Antwone's chest.Jim then eased his tongue towards Antwone's pecks,sucking both Antwone and the womans chest as he masturbated.

Markus rubbed his man part across Antwone's neck and face,while Duane stroked himself slowly.Antwone's eyes twitched,as he forced himself to stay in his right mind.Is he ok? the woman questioned,slightly concerned with Antwone's wellbeing.Yea,dont worry about him,just do your job,Duane ordered.

Fuck her Jim,Markus spoke as he kissed Antwone on the neck.

Jim placed the woman on the floor,spreading her legs open.Jim then fitted a condom on his hard prick and then placed himself inside the woman,pushing back and forth.

Fuck that bitch! Markus shouted.

Go fuck that nigga,while he fucking her,Markus ordered Antwone.Markus guided Antwone towards Jim and the woman.Jim's backside flexed as he continued to push himself into the woman.

Let me see how well you can fuck baby boy,Jim whispered as he turned his head towards Antwone.You like watching me fuck this bitch,Jim grunted as he pushed in and out of the womans fleshy tunnel.

Markus placed a condom on Antwone's prick and then pushed him towards Jim's backside.Antwone was high,but Jim's round rear end slightly got him aroused.Antwone began to stiffen and then placed himself inbetween Jim's buns.

Antwone shoved his huge erect prick back and forth into Jim as Jim moaned.

Markus gently slapped Antwone on the backside as Antwone continued to thrust into Jim.Markus then joined in,shoving his man part into Jim's mouth as

Antwone continued to dig into Jim.Jim enjoyed every minute of the activities,still grinding his prick into the woman.

Antwone stood on his toes,going deeper into Jim.

Antwone began to push faster,feeling Jim's inner muscles tighten around his hard prick.Antwone kept pushing himself into Jim,until he shot out,exploding into Jim,deep moans releasing from his full lips.

Antwone then pulled himself out of Jim,spanking Jim's behind with his still erect condom covered prick.

That was some good ass,wasn't it,Markus chuckled,pulling himself from Jim's mouth.

This nigga probably versatile,i think that's what they call it? Markus grinned.I dont get into all that gay slang,Markus explained.Antwone leaned his head on Jim's back,exhausted.

Antwone then sat on the couch,resting for thirty minutes as he watched the others.Duane headed towards Antwone,pulling Antwone to his feet.Duane began to kiss Antwone and then pushed Antwone towards the woman,wanting Antwone to fornicate with her.

My name is Jasmine,dont be shy,the woman whispered.

Jasmine pulled Antwone on top of her,pushing him inside her.Duane pushed himself into Antwone as Antwone pushed himself into Jasmine.The threesome lasted for forty minutes.

Duane sprayed himself over Antwone's back as Antwone poured himself inside of Jasmine.Antwone pulled himself out of Jasmine,witnessing the broken condom on the tip of his manhood.

The condom had ripped,unable to withstand the intense friction nor the size of Antwone's prick.Antwone had unknowingly spilled himself inside of Jasmine.

Antwone was mortified,but the drugs kept him mellow.Dont trip honey,i'll get that fixed,Jasmine whispered,meaning abortion,if she became pregnant.Antwone exhaled and then fell to the floor,sleeping like a baby for five hours.

Chapter 17

Antwone awoke,his naked body covered in man fluids.Antwone was back to his senses,examining his soaked and sticky body with disappointment.

Markus and Jim began to laugh,seeing Antwone's facial expression.

Antwone had a slight migraine,caused by the wild night of drugs and sex.

Duane and his friends were used to this kind of behavior.

Everyone was fully clothed again with the exception of Antwone.Let me help you,Jasmine whispered as she helped Antwone to the bathroom.Your not used to this shit,are you? Jasmine whispered as she helped Antwone wash himself up.

No,not really,Antwone responded silently.Antwone took one aleve pill,wanting his migraine to stop.You better stop popping them pills sweetheart,unless you want to become addicted,Jasmine chuckled.

I only take pills when i need them,Antwone smiled.

I put on a pair of your pants and your shirt,do you mind? Jasmine whispered.It's cool,Antwone laughed.Antwone placed on fresh clothes and then headed back into the living room.

There were four men in the living room,Duane,Markus,Jim and another strange man.The man had entered while Antwone was in the other room getting dressed.The man was draped in a dark coat,dark pants and a white shirt,wearing a pair of shades over his eyes.

Duane and the others stared at the man with fear.

Your wife told me that you would have the rest of my money,now pay up man or things are going to get ugly in this bitch,the man explained calmly to Duane.

What money? Duane questioned in fear.

Your wife brought a couple of kilos from me a few days ago,but she only paid me half price,but she told me you would pay the other half with interest,she told me she would keep her word,but i aint get my motherfucking money yet,the man explained angrily.

I didn't know anything about this shit? Duane explained quickly.

You know now nigga,now get the money man,this aint no game,the man explained.Im a old school nigga,either you get my money or somebody getting a cap busted in their ass,the man explained,his patients running thin.

Are you a new seller or some shit,because we usually buy from Jay,What's your name? Markus questioned the man timidly.

It's Bruce,but why the fuck is that any of your concern? Duane and his junky ass wife know who i am,that's all that matters,Bruce spoke as he pulled a gun from his coat pocket.

Bruce cocked his gun.

Bruce meant business,wearing shades to protect his identity,in case things got messy.Ya'll think im playing?! Bruce shouted.Nah man,but listen,this doesn't have anything to do with us,Markus explained eagerly,trying to sway Bruce from spilling any blood.

You right,so why am i having this conversation with you? Bruce

frowned,aiming his gun at Markus,pulling the trigger without hesitation.The bullet hit Markus directly in the head,ending his life quickly.

Blood rushed from the bullet wound,soaking the collar of Markus's shirt as he fell to the couch.

Jasmine screamed in fear,after witnessing Markus's death.Shut the hell up girl or you'll be next,Bruce explained silently.Damn man! Jim cried out,after seeing his longtime friend Markus put to death.

You'll be seeing that nigga soon,in the after life,Bruce said calmly,now aiming his gun towards Jim.

Nah man! Please dont do it dude,Jim begged.Jim's begging came to an end,once Bruce's bullet exited his gun,hitting Jim inbetween the eyes,putting Jim's life to rest.

Jim fell to the couch,next to Markus.Both Jim and Markus were dead,Duane was the only one in his group still alive,while his friends laid lifeless on the couch.

Nigga that's cold hearted man,Duane explained after witnessing the death of his friends.

That was just a motherfucking warning,i made your homeboys into examples,Bruce said with a blank expression,his face emotionless.This is all i have man,take it and leave,Duane said,handing Bruce eight hundred dollars from his wallet.

This aint shit,make this a thousand and you'll be redeemed nigga,Bruce ordered.

Im going to count to ten,you better have the rest,before i reach ten dude,Bruce explained.One,Two,Three,Bruce counted.Wait! Antwone shouted,interrupting Bruce before he reached the number four.

I can give you the rest,Antwone explained to Bruce,heading towards his bedroom.

Nah! Keep your ass right there,nigga you think im stupid,your ass was going in there for a gun,keep your ass next to that female,i know that's something you dont wanna do,faggot ass nigga,i know the shit Duane do,he fuck men and women,ya'll two are his whores,Bruce chuckled.

No,i do have money,Antwone explained.Antwone was willing to use the money in his safe to save Duane,but Bruce assumed Antwone was lying.

Turn towards your whores Duane,Bruce whispered,referring to Antwone and Jasmine.This is for making me wait for my motherfucking money,Bruce whispered as he shot Duane in the right arm.Duane yelled in pain as he held his arm.

Give me a chance to pay you back man! Duane pleaded.

And this is for making me come all this motherfucking way,Bruce chuckled as he shot Duane in his other arm.

Duane began to scream in pain even louder,after being shot in both of his arms.Duane fell to his knees,holding his arms as blood poured from the wounds.Antwone watched in fear as his stepfather yelled in pain.Bruce wanted to torture Duane before finishing him.

Tears fell from Duane's eyes as he stared into Antwone's eyes.

Duane's eyes penetrated deeply into Antwone's,he knew this was his last chance to apologize for all of his bad deeds.Im sorry Antwone,for everything dude,you was still willing to help me out,even tho i treated you like shit at times,that's gangsta,stay cool son,Duane gasped,those were Duane's last words.

Bruce placed the barrel of his gun in the back of Duane's head,firing one bullet into Duane's skull.The bullet traveled and pierced through Duane's major nerves,shooting through his forehead,killing Duane instantly.

Chapter 18

Duane's lifeless body fell to the floor as blood rushed from his head,staining the carpet.

That's what happens to fools,fools who dont pay their debts,Bruce frowned as he set his eyes on Antwone.Tears rushed from Antwone's eyes,seeing his stepfather lay dead,just a couple of inches away from his feet.

Duane was far from perfect,but Antwone still showed sympathy Towards

Duane's death,knowing him for almost his entire life.

Jasmine had curled herself into a corner,crying silently as she and Antwone witnessed the death toll increase.Take me to the money you claim to have,if you lying about it,shit aint going to end well for you homey,Bruce explained to Antwone.

Antwone headed towards his room,as Bruce followed behind him,pointing his gun at Antwone's back.

Antwone placed his arm under his bed,reaching for the safe,but felt something else brush across his arm,it was a pistol,the same pistol that he had removed from his mothers fingers.

Antwone had hid the gun under his bed,before the ambulance had arrived for his mother Pam.What's taking you so long? Get the fucking money,Bruce spoke as he pushed his gun into Antwone's back.Antwone was tempted to reach for the pistol,but grabbed the safe instead.

Bruce snatched the safe from Antwone's hands,before Antwone could hand it to him.

Wheres the fucking key? Bruce questioned.Bruce took his attention off of Antwone and then placed his gun towards the safes lock,blowing it off with a twitch of his finger.The lock shattered,falling to the floor as the safes door flew open,revealing thousands of dollars.

The safe contained Twenty thousand dollars and two pictures.

Antwone quickly pushed his hand under his bed again,his fingers wrapping around the pistol.Antwone quickly pulled the pistol from under the bed,into full view,aiming it at Bruce.

Bruce flinched,but then began to laugh.Nigga you dont have it in you,Bruce chuckled deeply.Leave man! Antwone explained as he continued to point the gun at Bruce.Bruce closed the safe and then set it on the bed,arrogantly aiming his gun at Antwone,knowing Antwone was nervous.

Die faggot,Bruce mumbled.Bruce grinned and then began to squeeze down on the trigger of his gun.

The phone rang,distracting Bruce from his original task,which was pulling the trigger of his gun.

Bruce wasn't the only one who lost concentration,so did Antwone.Antwone accidentally pulled the trigger of the pistol,being startled by the loud ringing phone.One bullet released from the tip of the pistol,shooting Bruce in the chest.

Bruce fell to the floor,holding his chest as blood rushed from his wound,his gun slipping from his fingers.Nah,not like this,Bruce choked out in deep pain.

Bruce squirmed on the floor,trying to resist the pain from his bullet wound.Bruce squirmed no more as his eyes shut,he could feel his life drain from his body.Bruce's heart stopped and so did the ringing phone.

Bruce was dead,his lifeless body resting on the floor of Antwone's bedroom.

Antwone quickly dropped the gun from his fingertips,he was traumatized by everything that had happened that night.Antwone curled himself up,next to his bed,two tears dropping from his eyes.Jasmine crept into the room,realizing it was too quiet.

Jasmine reached for Antwone's phone,calling the police as she comforted the silent Antwone.

The police arrived within minutes.Jasmine and Antwone explained everything to the police.Antwone watched as the four dead bodies were carried out of the house on stretchers,fully covered in body bags.

Chapter 19

Duane and his friends demons had finally caught up to them,and so did Bruce's.Death had took them all,Duane,Markus,Jim and Bruce.

The police asked Antwone and Jasmine a few more questions as they collected evidence.

Antwone gathered his things and some of his mothers things and then headed to his mothers parked car,after questioning,about to check into a hotel.Jasmine gently tapped on the car window,wanting to speak with Antwone.

Antwone slid the window down.

Can i get a ride? Jasmine questioned silently.Yea,sure,Antwone answered quietly.Thank's,Jasmine replied silenty as she entered the car.Antwone pulled off into the night.

You can drop me off right here,Jasmine whispered as she and Antwone drove up to a small townhouse.

Can i have your number? Jasmine questioned Antwone nervously.Shit like this should bring people closer together,we should keep in touch,Jasmine explained silently.Yea,i feel you,Antwone responded,speaking his number out.

Jasmine flipped open her cell phone,making a copy of Antwone's phone number.There was a picture of Jasmine and another woman kissing on the lips,set as Jasmine's screensaver.Who is that? Antwone questioned softly.That's my girlfriend,we have been together for two years now,Jasmine smiled.

Cool,Antwone smiled back.I never had a serious relationship,although i fooled around with this one dude at my school when i was seventeen,no sex,just touching and kissing really,Antwone chuckled.

Your gay too,Jasmine smiled.

Yea,Antwone answered.How were you able to,you know,get off then,Jasmine chuckled.I was thinking about dudes the whole time,Antwone replied with a grin.Antwone and Jasmine both laughed out.I do the same thing,i think about chicks tho,Jasmine smiled.We got a lot in common then,Jasmine laughed as she placed her phone back into her pocket.My father is gay too,talk about father like daughter,he even married his dude,they are so cute together,but they seemed sad,when i first met them.

My father and his husband knows what i do for a living,but they still treat me like family.They even offered me a place to stay,but i refused,i like doing my own thing,Jasmine smirked.

My fathers husband seems like the paternal type,he treated me like his own,i still keep in touch with them tho,Jasmine smiled.

My mother got pregnant with me before my father and his husband started dating.My father didn't know about me,my mother was just an experiment,something he tried out when they were drunk,my mother is honest,she holds nothing back,Jasmine chuckled.

My mother tells me to call my father Eddie,because i never grew up around him,but i still call him and his husband dad,Jasmine explained.

So,i'll see you around kid,Jasmine smiled and waved as she exited the car.Peace out,Antwone responded as he waved back at Jasmine,driving off.

Antwone headed to a hotel that night,renting a room for a week.

Antwone headed to his hotel room,placing all of his belongings in a pile,in a corner,sitting his money filled safe on top.Antwone's cell phone rang.He answered swiftly,placing the phone to his ear.

Hello,Antwone answered silently.

Hello Antwone,this is doctor Nicholas,I tried to reach you at the other number that you gave us,but no one answered,im sorry to inform you that your mother Pam has passed away,the doctor said quietly,feeling compassion for Antwone.

Antwone almost dropped the phone,after hearing those words.

She's dead? Antwone murmured silently as he held his tears back.Yes sir,we tried everything,there was just too much in her system,she was resuscitated,but her body finally gave in,sorry for your lost,the doctor whispered.

Thank's for notifying me,Antwone spoke,as tears rushed from his eyes.Antwone ended the call,throwing his cell phone into his pillow with force,angered and saddened with the news he received.If Antwone had thrown his cell phone somewhere else other than the pillow it would have probably broken,after being thrown with force and rage.Antwone's tears soaked the hotel bed and his clothes as he cried that entire night.

Chapter 20

Antwone buried his mother and Duane a week later.

Antwone paid his respects at both funerals,crying and drinking himself to sleep every night,after the funerals took place.Antwone had rented the hotel room for another two weeks,trying to place his shattered life back together,piece by piece.

Antwone became more focused in his third week,bringing his drinking and depression to a minimum.

Antwone thought of useful ways to use some of his savings.Antwone headed out the next morning,searching for his long lost family.Antwone and his recently deceased mother and stepfather had lived in a remote location,which would make it hard for people to track them.

Antwone could remember small bits and pieces of his father and his family,leaving him with tearful nights.

Antwone headed to Wood Lake Springs,hearing his mother and Duane talk about the town,a long time ago,when they thought he wasn't listening.Antwone purchased a foreclosed cottage within the town,while he visited,in search of his other family.

Antwone became slightly adjusted to his new home,after eight and a half months of living there alone.

Antwone decided to leave his home for awhile,wanting to investigate the town a little more,and grab something to eat,while he was out.Antwone stopped at the local diner,ordering a cup of tea and toast.

My gosh! You look so familiar?! The waitress shouted in a clear voice as she examined Antwone.Where have i seen you before? The waitress questioned Antwone silently.

I used to live here,when i was a kid,but i haven't been here in nearly fifteen years or more,im not really sure,Antwone smiled.The waitress smiled back.Wait! Are you related to the neilson family?

The waitress questioned,awaiting Antwone's answer.

Yea! I am,Antwone answered,hoping he had found someone who could give him some answers.

What's your full name? The waitress questioned silently.Antwone Neilson! Antwone spoke.I knew i recognized that cute face,your father used to bring you here on occasions,you have grownup to be so handsome,The waitress grinned.

You have been the talk of the town for many years,your father and grandfather and your stepfather have been looking for you since the day you went missing,The waitress explained.

Go to this place called the AAA bathhouse,you might find your folks there,im not sure if your into the things that happen there,but your folks own it,The waitress explained politely.

Thank's mam,Antwone smiled,as he raised from the table,leaving a twenty dollar tip.

No problem honey,but you haven't touched your toast or tea? The waitress explained silently.I guess he in a rush,the waitress chuckled as she placed the tip in her bra.

Antwone headed to the AAA bathhouse,but found none of his family on that day,although he found another youngman who caught his interest.The youngman had a smooth dark caramel brown complexion and lips that could make you melt,and short wavy thick hair,His name was Mike,he and Antwone complimented each other very well.

Antwone continued with his search,with assistance from Mike.

Antonio and Eddie,including Anthony rarely visited the AAA after Antwone's absence,only participating in the business part,but never taking time out to relax the way they used to,People rarely saw them,as time passed by,only on occasions,but nobody knew their whereabouts.

Chapter 21

Two weeks had passed.

Antwone slipped into his depression again,starting to lose hope,not knowing if he would ever see his family again,even tho he was so close to finding them.

Antwone visited the AAA again,hoping to find some traces of his family.No one knew anything,not even the employee who worked the front desk.They come in early,before i get here,they handle all of the scheduling,the money,the merchandise,and the cleaning,i just welcome all the hot guys in,and closeup at the end of the day,an employee of the AAA answered,after being questioned by Antwone.

Thank's,please let me know if you hear anything from them,Antwone pleaded to the man.

Sure thing,the man replied.

Antwone decided to explore the AAA bathhouse before leaving,hoping that would give him some kind of connection with his long lost family.Antwone took a long shower,all of his memories surging through his head,the bad and the good.

Antwone finished his shower and then wrapped a towel around his waist,he then slipped his feet into a pair of flip flops,heading into one of the vacant rooms.Antwone grabbed a bottle of oil from the cupboard,massaging the oil into his smooth brown skin,sitting on a bench.

Antwone relaxed himself,relieving any stress he had.

A man entered the room,his skin as brown as Antwone's,his lips full,his sculpture similar to Antwone's.The man was an older man,but was well groomed and maintained for his age.

You new here? If you're looking for some good action,go check out room six,the man spoke politely to Antwone,not staring Antwone directly in the face.

Nah,im talking to someone at the moment,not really looking for any hookups,just came in here to relax,i've been kind of stressed lately,Antwone replied.I understand,i get that way myself sometimes,the man answered in his deep voice.

The man sat beside Antwone,relaxing his muscles.

So,where is your boyfriend? The man questioned Antwone.He's not really my boyfriend,but we have an arrangement,Antwone explained.Oh,i see,one of those,you have an open relationship,the man chuckled.

Yea,pretty much,Antwone smiled.

You have a nice body,the man whispered to Antwone.Likewise,Antwone smirked.Antwone and the man both adjusted their towels,feeling slight sexual tension between them.

Since you and your boyfriend have an open relationship i guess it would be ok for me to do this,the man said as he pushed his lips onto Antwone's.Antwone and the man lip locked for a minute,until the man finally focused on Antwone's face,instead of his body.

Damn! You favor my son,the man said silently.What's your last name? The man questioned Antwone with curiosity.Neilson,Antwone spoke.

Neilson! Damn,i hope i aint kissed my own nephew or little cousin,the man exhaled.Are you related to Charlie Neilson? That's my younger brother,the man explained.

Yea,I come from the Neilson bloodline,but my father is Antonio,do you know him? Antwone explained quietly,awaiting the mans response.

The man froze in place,as if he seen a ghost.Im Antonio's father,which makes me your grandfather! The man explained,as his eyes widened,guilt sweeping his face,now knowing he shared an intimate and lust filled kiss with his long lost grandson.

Chapter 22

Antwone and the man didn't know that they were related at the time they kissed,but they were soon taking over by tears of joy.Antwone! Is that your name? The man questioned,impatiently waiting for an answer,trying to reaffirm that the youngman was his grandson.

Yea,Antwone spoke,his nerves rushing through his body.Im Anthony Neilson! Come here man! It's nothing but love here little man,do you know how much we have missed you dude? Anthony trembled,tears rushing down his face.

Anthony kissed Antwone repeatly on both cheeks,hugging Antwone tightly.

Im sorry,i forgot that you aint no kid anymore,Anthony apologized for his tight hugs and kisses.I just really missed you baby boy,you a Neilson,it's a piece of me in you,Anthony gasped,trying to stop his tears.

It's cool,i understand,it's been so long,Antwone cried out.Man i lost ya'll,i lost my mother,things have been hard,but im back,Antwone smiled as tears fell from his eyes.

Antwone and Anthony forgot about the kiss they shared,being overpowered by their emotions,wanting to know everything that has been going on in each others lives.Someone else entered the room as Antwone and Anthony made up for lost time.

Antonio? I thought you was in the other room sleeping? Eddie spoke softly,referring to Antwone.

This aint Antonio,this Antwone,Anthony chuckled,his eyes red and watery.Antwone! Dude you lying man,that's little a? Eddie said silently.Yea,this is his little ass,he big A now,Anthony smirked,brushing the tears from his eyes.

Antwone! Look at me,Eddie demanded.

Eddie quickly turned his head the other way,trying not to stare Antwone directly in the eyes,not wanting Antwone and Anthony to see him cry.Im going to go get your pops,Eddie spoke silently,as tears flowed down his face,Eddie still tried and struggled to maintain his tough guy image.

Eddie brought Antonio to the room.

Antonio entered the room slowly,his eyes locking on Antwone.Antwone's eyes watered as he examined his father.Antonio stood quietly at the door,staring his lookalike in the eyes,tears began to slowly pour down Antonio's face.

Antonio wrapped his arms tightly around Antwone,as they both released long streams of tears from their eyes.

I love you man,Antonio whispered to Antwone as they held on to each other,not letting go.

Eddie moved closer to Antonio and Antwone as they hugged,his eyes red and watery.Im not letting you go again,Antonio explained to Antwone.Im here forever this time,Antwone whispered.

Your dad aint never letting you go,not this time,from father to son,keep them words in your head Antwone,you the fruit of my loins man,Antonio muttered,as he and Antwone continued to tightly embrace,tears soaking their bodies and towels.

Eddie could not ignore his emotions any longer,joining in the father and son hug,his tears combining with theirs.We been missing you Antwone,Eddie murmured silently,allowing his emotions to pour out as he kept his arms tightly around Antwone and Antonio.

Anthony joined in also,wrapping his arms around them all,his son,grandson and son in law.They all tightly embraced each other,tears hitting their smooth chests and then their navels and then their towels and then their flip flops,it was a human fountain.

They were all reunited again.

Chapter 23

Antwone's potential boyfriend entered the room,seeing the four men united together.You finally found them! Mike murmured to Antwone from the sidelines,seeing the tears in the mens eyes,knowing that Antwone had finally found his long lost family.

Mike examined the four men closely,seeing the resemblance between Antwone and his father and grandfather,the three of them could be each others clones.

This is them,Antwone spoke silently,twitching his finger towards Mike,wanting him to join the group hug.

Mike readjusted his towel and then joined the group.

This is my friend Mike,me and him got a little something going on,Antwone chuckled silently.Join the team baby boy,we all homos,Anthony chuckled deeply as everyone else did.

Antwone's laughter ended after his cell phone began to ring,being distracted from his small family reunion.Antwone grabbed his cell phone from the cupboard he placed it in.

Hello,Antwone answered as he departed from the circle.It's Jasmine Antwone,your stepsister! Jasmine chuckled.I thought you looked familiar,you favored the little boy in the pictures with my dad and Antonio,both my dads,Jasmine corrected.

So i started asking questions and i found out that the boy in the pictures name was Antwone too,Jasmine explained.I called you plenty of times,but you never answered your phone,Jasmine said quietly.

I told our fathers eventually,i told our fathers everything,about us,and Duane,and everything else that went down,Jasmine murmured.

They wanted to fuck Duane up,im serious,especially after i told them Duane got it on with you,Jasmine chuckled.I knew you would go searching for them at that bathhouse,so i told them to keep a lookout,Jasmine explained as an infant baby cried in the background.

So that's why they were here,an employee told me that they didn't come here much anymore,Antwone whispered.Dont be mad Antwone,but i got news for you,Jasmine spoke timidly.What news? You can tell me,we family now,Antwone spoke softly.

Boy dont be mad at me,but my girlfriend and me really thought about having a baby and starting a new life,so once i found out i had got pregnant,from that night,you remember,the night the condom broke,Jasmine chuckled silently.

Jasmine had became pregnant,after taking in Antwone's seed,months ago.

Jasmine had once thought of abortion,but became attached to the growing baby in her womb,changing her mine completely.I wanted something new in my life,you gave me that,so thank you,and yea,the baby is yours,Jasmine explained.

He's yours,Jasmine chuckled again,revealing the babys gender.

I heard your grandfather likes A names,so how about Aidan? Jasmine questioned Antwone,awaiting his approval.Im a father? And you my stepsister? What the fuck? Antwone chuckled.I cant believe this,i dont even know if im father material? Antwone gasped nervously with a smile.You'll get used to it,just give him an A name,that's a start,Jasmine laughed.

Okay,how about Anthony Neilson,the second? Antwone spoke.

Perfect,that's going to be this boys name then,Jasmine responded.Im about to send you a picture,he's gorgeous,ya'll Neilson's got some strong genes,Jasmine laughed out.Alright,send it,Antwone smiled.

Jasmine snapped a quick photo of the newborn,sending it to Antwone's phone.

Antwone received the picture in seconds,getting his first glance of his newborn son Anthony Neilson the second.

The baby was completely healthy,with features that resembled his father Antwone,and his grandfather and great grandfather.The baby also favored Eddie,who was his grandfather and step grandfather.

The young Anthony Neilson the second resembled an angel as Jasmine cradled his small naked brown body in her warm arms.

Antwone smiled proudly,his emotions growing even stronger,already feeling a connection with the young child as he examined the photo.I have to breastfeed him a lot,apparently he's a breast man,but who knows? He might be joining ya'll circle soon.Once you come down here and sign his birth certificate,you can hold him yourself,my titties hurt,Jasmine chuckled.

We can get joined custody too,if you cool with it? Jasmine explained to Antwone.I didn't meet Eddie until i was grown,i dont want Anthony to go through that,so it would mean a lot to me if he knew you,and spent time with you,like a child and their father or mother should,Jasmine cried.Yea,im cool with it,I know where your coming from,trust me,it's new to me,but i'll definitely be in Anthony's life,Antwone said with conviction,wanting to raise Anthony the second,and watch him grow into a man,helping him with his life choices,and loving him,that was the most important part.Tell our fathers their grandchild is here,later little brother,Jasmine chuckled,ending the call afterwards.

Come here for a second,Jasmine had the baby,Antwone called out to his family.Antwone showed everyone the picture of Anthony Neilson,the second.

Damn Antonio,we grandparents man,Eddie chuckled,getting a warm feeling inside.We got a grandchild together dude,Eddie smiled at Antonio.I know,im still in shock,Antonio responded with a wide smile.

Antonio and Eddie were now linked together by more than their strong marriage,but by Anthony the second also,both of them being baby Anthony the seconds biological grandfathers.

Im a great grandfather now,damn im getting old,Anthony chuckled.We have a new member of the family,Antonio smiled.Yes indeed,Eddie chuckled.Anthony Neilson the second,i like the way that sounds,Anthony grinned.

I got a son now,i hope that's cool with you? Antwone whispered to Mike.

It's very cool with me,i got a son too,his name is Mikey,i had him with this girl i used to mess with,before i began to date dudes only,i was waiting until we got serious to tell you about him,Mike whispered back to Antwone.

If things go smooth with us,we can raise them together,Mike smiled,wrapping his arms around Antwone.That would be cool,Antwone replied silently.

Antwone turned back towards his father Antonio,he and Antonio's eyes watering once more as they embraced again.Antwone,Antonio,Anthony and Eddie were all reunited again,at last,but they gained a few new members to their family.

The whole family exploded into laughter as they all hugged again.The AAA bathouse was filled with their laughter and tears,their family was intact once more,not for a portion of time,but forever,as long as they lived.And beyond,because their love and family bond was eternal.

The end.

Epilogue: The AAA's story had ended,which was short for Anthony,Antonio and Antwone.

But a new A had been born,which was Anthony the second,and his story would continue the saga.But the old saga would live forever in memories.

Twenty years had passed.

Anthony the second had grew over the years,becoming a handsome youngman,and so did Mikey.Antonio and Mike's relationship had intensified,they had gotten married and raised Anthony the second and Mikey together as brothers,as they said they would.

Anthony the second and Mikey were browsing through a photo book of old family photos as they laid side by side in a secluded room at the AAA bathhouse naked,with nothing but short white towels around their waists.

There was a photo of Pam and Duane,holding Antwone,in happier times,when they weren't fighting.And another picture of Anthony the first,Antonio,Antwone and Eddie,a picture tooken before Antwone was taken away from his now reunited family.

There was another picture that caught Anthony the second and Mikey's attention,an innocent picture of them being given a bubble bath together,by their two fathers,when they were children.

They both smirked as they examined the picture.

Anthony the second and Mikey's bubble baths together didn't stop,after they grew into adulthood.Anthony the second and Mikey's brotherly love had developed into more of a romantic and intimate relationship.

Anthony the second and Mikey became each others romantic interests,once hitting puberty,discovering new and intense sensations,finding new substances exiting from their male organs,substances they splashed each other in,after their physical experiments together.

Anthony the second and Mikey headed out of the room,placing the photo book in a cupboard as they exited the room.Anthony II and Mikey worked most weekends at the AAA.And were well paid.Anthony II and Mikey were in charge of cleaning,mopping and sterilizing the AAA,and closingup.

Anthony II and Mikey placed on a pair of running shoes,wanting to protect their feet,not bothering to put on any clothes,but still kept the towels around their waists.Anthony II and Mikey were very liberated and somewhat nudists.

Anthony II and Mikey headed out of the AAA,locking up,after they exited.Mikey tucked the keys to the AAA inside of his running shoes,he and Anthony II having nowhere else to put them,them being practically naked.

Anthony II ran into the forest with Mikey chasing behind him.

Mikey followed behind Anthony II,infatuated and seduced by Anthony II's smooth and sculpted body,tracing Anthony II's fresh scent deeper into the woods.There was a specific spot

Anthony II and Mikey went to within the forest.

The trees were tall,the ground was covered with green grass and many plants.Anthony II owned most of the land,just like all of Anthony I's descendants.

Mikey forcefully grabbed Anthony II's waist,kissing him gently.The kiss Anthony II and Mikey shared was filled with intense passion,almost orgasmic.Anthony II and Mikey were deeply connected to each other,this was something they kept secret,only between the two of them,but Anthony I knew about the love affair brewing between the two young men,but thought it was best to keep it to himself,until they announced it themselves.

The news would be shocking when they announced it to their family,but wouldn't have any negative effect on their unbreakable family bond.

Anthony II and Mikey continued with their passionate kiss,as their tongues joined the action.We have been coming here for the past three years dude,we might as well tell our folks what's up Anthony,Mikey explained as he untied his lips from Anthony II's,becoming tired of hiding his feelings for Anthony II.

Let's wait,at least until we finish school,Anthony II insisted,slightly afraid of the reaction he and Mikey would receive from their two fathers and the rest of their family.

Why is Ben always asking you to help him with his homework,when the nigga got a 3.0 gpa? Mikey questioned with a frown.Wait! Is that why you always getting into it with him,trying to start some mess with him? Anthony II questioned silenty.Nah! But im just saying Anthony,dude act like he got a thing for you and that shit aint cool,Mikey spoke,jealousy in his voice.

Mikey you my stepbrother dude,what we doing aint cool,Anthony II spoke,with a serious facial expression.

You think i dont know that man? Mikey explained angrily.You knew what we was getting into dude,but you never once tried to end it,you grown,just tell me to back off,Mikey spoke silently,his eyes meeting Anthony II's.

Dont act like you dont want me either dude,you said you had feelings for me Anthony,Mikey said quietly.You love me dude? Mikey questioned Anthony II.Anthony II became quiet.I told you i had feelings for you Mikey,what else do you wanna hear man? Anthony spoke silently,not wanting to confess his true desires for Mikey.

Just answer the question man,Do you love me? Mikey questioned again,pushing himself closer to Anthony II.

I love you as a brother man,nothing more,Anthony II spoke softly,not being completely honest.

Then why are we going through this Anthony? Huh,why are we up here in these woods and mountains and shit? Doing shit brothers shouldn't be doing,If you claim to only love me like a brother?

Mikey explained,his eyes becoming watery.

Why do your dick get all hard when we fooling around with each other,if you love me like a brother? Mikey questioned as his lips headed towards Anthony II's.

You entered this relationship voluntarily Anthony,just like me,Mikey spoke in a low tone.Mikey gently pushed Anthony II against a tree,pushing his well built body onto Anthony II's.Mikey began to caress Anthony II's abdomen and pecks,leaning his forehead into Anthony II's.

Anthony II gently pushed Mikey away from him.

What are you fighting me for Anthony?! Mikey shouted,his rod becoming stiff.Nigga you letting your hormones get the best of you,you dont love me dude,Anthony II spoke,trying to resist his urges.

If i didn't love you,then why the fuck was i crying when i thought it was you who was in that car accident back at school,Mikey explained himself,in his deep voice.Im in love and in lust with you dude,Mikey explained calmly.

Anthony II became speechless.

I do love you dude,but this shit is scary man,what we doing is considered a taboo,Anthony II said,admitting his love for Mikey.

That's all i wanted to hear man,for you to admit you caught feelings for me dude,Mikey spoke softly.We came out here for a reason,Mikey smirked,wanting to break the ice,and begin one on one activities with Anthony II,activities that were for grownups,like him and Anthony II.Anthony II smiled.

The warm air didn't make Anthony II and Mikey feel uncomfortable about being in nothing but towels and a pair of running shoes.

Anthony II kneeled to the ground,pulling his hand underneath Mikey's towel,reaching for Mikey's man part.Anthony II began to stroke Mikey's equipment back and forth,as Mikey moaned out.

Anthony II then pulled his hand underneath his own towel,stroking himself as he devoured Mikey's rod.

That's what's up! Suck that shit baby! Mikey moaned deeply from the pleasure he received from Anthony II.Anthony II began to create a deep suction with his throat as he continued to swallow Mikey's rod.Mikey began to moan louder as the pleasure intensified greatly.

Mikey's voice was very deep and clear,if they were in the AAA,many people would hear them.But they weren't,they were in the woods.

Oh fuck! Take it out your mouth dude! Im about to bust,Mikey quickly explained,not wanting the pleasure to be over yet.

Dude you wanted me to cum in your mouth or something? Mikey moaned,after quickly exiting Anthony II's mouth,not ready to succumb to his lust for Anthony II,wanting he and Anthony

II's activities to last.Mikey pulled Anthony II to his feet,kissing him on the lips.Nigga you like having power over me,dont you? Mikey grinned,as his full lips departed from Anthony II's.Nigga bend your ass over,let me try something on you,Mikey whispered in Anthony II's ear,before bending him over.

Anthony II's rear poked up,as Mikey gently pushed Anthony II's head near the tree.

Mikey kneeled down,pushing his head underneath Anthony II's towel,about to push his face inbetween Anthony II's buns.Anthony II could feel Mikey's lips touch his bare backside.Man you nasty,we ain't never tried nothing like this before,Anthony II explained.

Nigga just stay calm and let me go to work,Mikey explained patiently as he stroked himself from underneath his towel,making Anthony II whimper.Mikey licked and kissed Anthony II up and down,as Anthony II continued to moan,his prick throbbing.

Mikey then stood to his feet,still stroking himself.

Anthony II was about to rise,but Mikey placed one of his big hands flat against Anthony II's back,pushing him back down.Keep that ass in the air nigga,i ain't done,im about to pound it,Mikey moaned.

Lift that towel and open that ass up nigga,spread them cheeks,Mikey demanded Anthony II in his deep manly voice.But we aint got no rubbers man,Anthony II explained.Damn! I wanna fuck it,that joint just waiting for me,Mikey spoke,eager to place himself inside of Anthony II.

Mikey placed his legs around Anthony II's,wrapping his arms around Anthony II's chest,massaging his extremely hard prick against Anthony II's posterior,without penetrating it,his head resting on the back of Anthony II's neck.Mikey continued to slide his hard prick inbetween Anthony II's buns,but did not enter,his prick becoming wet at the tip,as the motion brought him closer and closer to a climax.

Once we get a condom,that ass is mine man,Mikey explained himself,trying his best not to push himself inside of Anthony II.

Spin back around man,all you doing is tempting me,Mikey spoke as he arose from Anthony II.

lay on the grass dude,Mikey commanded Anthony II,as he did the same.Mikey placed his crotch towards Anthony II's face,as he leaned his head towards Anthony II's crotch.You do me and i'll do you,Mikey explained quietly to Anthony II.They both began to slowly gulp down each others man parts.The position lasted for twenty five minutes.

Mikey and Anthony II stood up again,groping and touching each other,trying out different physical activities.

Mikey placed Anthony II on his knees,slapping his hung and well equipped man part across Anthony II's face as Anthony II stroked himself from the slit in his towel.

Mikey grabbed Anthony II by the hips,placing Anthony II on the soft grass.Mikey placed Anthony II's legs around his waist,towering over Anthony II in the process,sliding both he and Anthony II's hardened pricks together from the slight openings in their towels.

Mikey began to push and massage his erect prick onto Anthony II's erect prick,their male organs intertwined like serpents,as they continued to grind intensely.Mikey and Anthony II's loins throbbed and pulsated in deep pleasure.Mikey and Anthony II's rods began to quiver and vibrate as they mingled together with intense friction and motion,giving Anthony II and Mikey extreme ecstasy.

Anthony II and Mikey began to kiss as they felt themselves about to achieve the sensation of a climax.

Mikey jumped to his feet,before he could shoot out.Mikey hovered over Anthony II,his toned thighs surrounding Anthony II's shoulders as Anthony II reached his hand towards Mikey's tight buttocks,grabbing and groping it.

Mikey and Anthony II stroked themselves harder and faster,as they focused on each other with fiery lust.

Anthony II and Mikey squirted each other with their hot and thick and white colored man fluids.Anthony II shot into the air,hitting the tip of Mikey's sack and hard rod,while Mikey shot himself on Anthony II's pecks and abs.

Anthony II and Mikey moaned and grunted in satisfaction.

Mikey let himself fall to the grass,beside Anthony II,his towel falling from his waist.Mikey and Anthony II's eyes flickered as they moaned in exhaustion and gratification,after their sexual activities and intense orgasms were over.

Mikey gave Anthony II a quick peck on the cheek as he wrapped his arms around Anthony II's waist,causing Anthony II's towel to fall from his hips.Anthony II and Mikey fell asleep,as the dim sunlight shined upon their wet naked flesh.

Anthony II and Mikey slept in the wilderness,until it was dark out.

Anthony II and Mikey awoke from their deep slumber,after the sun had went down,placing their towels back around their waists as they slowly walked home,watching the stars in the night sky.

Being a same sex oriented and career focused male seemed like a family tradition in the Neilson family,a tradition that seemed to spread to each generation without explanation.

Anthony II was the fourth Neilson male to be given a name that started with the letter A,and the second to have the name Anthony.Anthony II and Mikey were about to start their own destiny together.

A new chapter was about to begin.